ENHANCE YOUR
PRESENCE

THE PATH TO PERSONAL POWER, PROFESSIONAL INFLUENCE & BUSINESS RESULTS

MARK J. TAGER, MD
ROBERT JOHN HUGHES

Praise for *Enhance Your Presence*

How do you exit an ocean of sameness and enter a small pool of distinction? This excellent book argues that your presence can create measurable impact and lasting influence. It defines what presence is and demonstrates it with substantive human examples. A good read. A solid resource.

Dr. Nido R. Qubein
President, High Point University
Chairman, Great Harvest Co

There's a "secret" to success in the corporate world. And it's a simple one. Be attentive. Be authentic. Be present. Many of the best decisions get made because the champion of an idea has the personal power and persuasive ability to inspire confidence. *Enhance Your Presence* reveals the secret as a series of actionable, practical steps that together create a fundamental shift in self-expression. This shift increases the likelihood of success.

Keith J. Krach
Chairman & CEO, DocuSign

A fantastic read! I read it straight though. *Enhance Your Presence* offers great insights into presenting from two authors who clearly know what they are talking about. Whether it is your first or your 1000th presentation, Mark and Robert provide valuable tips and pearls for improving your ability to clearly communicate a message. Regardless if you are standing in front of a classroom, boardroom, lecture hall, camera or computer screen, I assure you that you will feel better prepared. *Enhance your Presence* should be mandatory for all those who frequently present their ideas. I learned a lot.

Steven Dayan, MD, FACS
NY Times Best Selling Author

Enhance Your Presence is a great reminder that self-awareness, attention and presence are gifts not only to one's self but also to others. Become present, stay present, live present and everything else will take care of itself.

Timothy P. Shriver, PhD
Chairman Special Olympics

Enhance Your Presence represents the foundation of how to connect with authenticity. It is a compelling, easy to follow playbook of influence in one on one conversations and filled auditoriums, alike. I found *Enhance Your Presence* to be, without a doubt, the most helpful guide I have seen in presenting and connecting for impact. Well done!

Stephen Beeson, MD
Founder, The Physician Effectiveness Project

I remember meeting Mark moments after he heard a presentation I gave. In about 3 minutes he summed up all the areas in which I could improve to make a bigger impact on my audience. This book is the perfect collection of his and Robert's knowledge, wisdom and passion. Each page is SPOT ON! *Enhance Your Presence* is powerful. It is practical. And these methods work. I literally could flip to any page and soak up another takeaway.

Leigh Weinraub, MA
Founder, Mind in Motion
Miraval Specialist

Mark and Robert provide a simple and effective framework for each of us to offer our gifts to the world. This book and its teachings remind me to open my heart and connect with my audience. Enhancing your presence is less about learning skills than it is about transformation. Read it, feel it, live it.

Patrick Hanaway, MD
Medical Director
Center for Functional Medicine, Cleveland Clinic

Training Academy

991 C Lomas Santa Fe Drive
Box 464
Solana Beach, CA 92015
www.changewell.com

ISBN-10: 0-9977231-0-6

ISBN-13: 978-0-9977231-0-6

Mark's Dedication:

To the woman who taught me the most about presence: my, Mother, Judith Tager. And to those who remind me about it every day: Carol, Marissa, Chloe and Sienna.

Robert's Dedication:

Nothing in my life happens without the love and support of my wife Pat who encourages me to find the balance between "too serious" and not serious enough. She is my editor in chief and contributed generously to crafting these words as well as to the design and functioning of our enterprise. This book is also dedicated to our family: Sally, Bryan, and Wyatt Biederman, Georgi Hughes, Louise Hughes and Al Nathanson.

Acknowledgements

Want to get something done well? Put it in the capable hands of the millennial generation. Heartfelt thanks to James Tager and Chelsea Davis, two gifted researchers and wordsmiths. Sean Willard, Clark Thompson, Abhijit Sarkar and our talented team of illustrators in India put the words into pages, and the pages into this illustrated book.

Mark draws enormous inspiration from his healthcare colleagues who have adopted an integrative framework that benefits both patients and clinicians alike.

Randy McNamara, Alan and Nancy Ross taught Robert the life changing distinctions of authenticity, self-expression and leadership. Mike Koenigs helped Robert with his first book and continues to demonstrate how to put online tools to work serving humanity.

Special thanks to John VerStandig, Ken and Linda Schatz, Franz and Sally Jaggar, Bill Moyes, Mark Ramsey, Mike Shepard, Nancy Wolfson, Marice Tobias, Rich Werges, Dick Zaragoza, Nick Oliva, Sandra Hewick, Troy Daum, Andreas Schenk, Bill Lerner, Richard Wolf and John Weston.

We are inspired by Ryan Deiss, Eben Pagan, Brendon Burchard, Jeff Walker, Dan Kennedy, Andy Jenkins, Mike Filsaime, and Tony Robbins, each of whom are brilliant examples of presence and servant leadership.

The authors are deeply thankful to the graduates of our *Enhance Your Presence Training*™ program who opened their minds and hearts to the possibility that presence can change the world.

Table of Contents

Foreword

From the moment I first met Dr. Mark Tager and Robert Hughes, I suspected there was something special and unique about them. Some people just have that air of confidence and assurance that makes you sit up and take notice. My intuition subsequently proved to be correct.

Enhance Your Presence is an interesting title for a book. Without the subtitle, it could take you in a number of directions. Seriously, who wouldn't want to enhance their presence? But are we talking about physical attractiveness, or communication capabilities, or mental acuity, or our personal aura? In fact, this book just might give you an advantage in all of these areas and more, as suggested in the subtitle: *The Path to Personal Power, Professional Influence, and Business Results.*

For the past several years I have been an ambassador and evangelist for Solutionreach, a medical software company that helps healthcare practices engage with their patients on a deeper level. I guide these practices in proactively reaching out to their patients and strengthening connections with them. I love how the concepts in this book are a perfect complement to what I have been preaching—an enhanced presence is an attainable goal for any medical practice. How better to retain existing patients, attract new patients, and ensure compliance? Patients have many choices regarding whom to turn to for their healthcare. Implementing a few well-thought-out strategies can make the difference between keeping a patient for life and losing them to a competitor. As I visit with key opinion leaders and healthcare partners, the message of this book is reinforced; an enhanced presence is the key to setting yourself apart, not only as an individual but—perhaps more importantly—as a vibrant and welcoming practice.

I enjoy watching TED talks. There's a magical quality to being able to condense your message into a succinct 18-minute window with no extraneous content. Done right, you can inform, educate, and entertain in this short time frame. But what is it that makes these talks memorable? Yes, the content is important, but in most cases it's the delivery that makes the difference, and it's the same in all aspects of our lives, both personally and professionally. This is where Mark and Robert shine. Having read their book, I now recognize the keys that previously were only subliminal. Why are some people fascinating to talk to? What is it that draws you to certain individuals? Why do some messages seem to resonate more deeply than others? There really is a difference between a good presentation and a great presentation, and anyone can learn the techniques. Once mastered, these simple concepts carry over to all aspects of your life. Thinking back, I recognize that this was what made the authors stand out to me when I first met them. They were a living testament to enhanced power, influence, and results.

Soon after my initial interaction with Mark and Robert I attended one of their ChangeWell Training Academy's *Enhance Your Presence* workshops in one of my favorite cities: San Diego. They claimed to have insights into proven methods of helping great speakers become exceptional. I considered myself to be an adequate speaker based on the positive feedback I had received at a number of meetings and symposia over the past several years. I had also recently been published in a medical marketing journal and felt that I was making a significant contribution as a representative of Solutionreach. Nonetheless, I knew I could do better, and I went into this training session with great anticipation and perhaps a bit of fear at the prospect of being put on the spot in front of a group of colleagues. Well, not only did I find a great sense of community that day; the concepts I learned have changed me forever.

I try to avoid spoiler alerts, so I'll just say that Robert and Mark are everything I thought they would be and more. This book is a compilation of the best of their insights on self-improvement. You'll uncover proven methods for becoming a better person and presenting yourself in the most positive light, whether it be from the podium, in a business setting, or in more intimate face-to-face interactions. It's analogous to the fine-tuning that makes the difference between a good athlete and a world-class competitor. I promise you that you'll enjoy this journey.

Ron Hartley
Business Relationship Manager
Solutionreach

Draper, Utah
June 20, 2016

Thanks for purchasing this edition of
Enhance Your Presence.

This book comes with a free video training course and other valuable downloads. It's our gift to you. Visit this link to get the content:

bit.do/changewell

Introduction:

The Challenge of Change

"If you aren't in over your head,
how do you know how tall you are?"
—T.S. Eliot

Once upon a time, in a small fairy-tale village in the Catskill Mountains of New York state, there lived a man named Rip Van Winkle. According to the 1819 Washington Irving short story, Mr. Van Winkle was a kindly man of Dutch descent, beloved by all in the village—especially children, because he told them funny stories. If he had a character flaw, it was that he hated to work. This bothered his wife to no end.

It was a peaceful time, just before the start of the American Revolution in 1775. One pleasant autumn afternoon, Rip Van Winkle went for a walk in the woods with his dog to get away from the cares of life and his nagging wife. On the way up a hill, he ran into a strangely dressed man struggling with a barrel of whiskey. He helped the man carry it. Soon enough, they came to a clearing where other men, dressed similarly in antiquated Dutch costumes, were bowling. Van Winkle joined in, playing the game and sampling the liquor. Eventually, he fell asleep under a tree.

When he awoke, 20 years had passed. Everything familiar about his life had changed. His beard was now a foot long; his rifle had rusted; his dog was gone; his wife had died; and King George III of England no longer ruled the land. Thanks to the American Revolution, George Washington was now America's first president.

After what had seemed like an afternoon's nap, Rip Van Winkle literally now lived in a different country, with new customs and rules. No one knew who he was. His old ideas no longer worked—in fact, they got him into trouble.

You haven't been asleep for the last 20 years. But in that period of time, no matter what profession, industry, or business you are in, everything about our world has changed. And it keeps changing at an ever-increasing pace. The results of these changes touch us all:

> *There are new rules that govern the process of conducting business and attracting and retaining customers, clients, and patients.*

Feeling the Growing Forces of Change

Let's start with perhaps the biggest changes. The World Wide Web was invented in 1989 and released for public use in 1993. AOL ("America Online") went public in 1991, eventually becoming a leading provider of e-mail services. Google was founded in 1998. By 2001, over half of all Americans were using the Internet. Facebook began in February 2004. The iPhone was released in July of 2007. It is hard to imagine that just 20 years ago, none of these information tools were widely known or used.

If you are a member of the millennial generation, born after 1980, you are a "digital native." It's as if you were born the day Rip Van Winkle fell asleep. What seems strange to him seems perfectly normal to you because you have never experienced any other way. Of course you would find restaurants, pay bills, make purchases, deposit checks, and make appointments using your mobile phone. Why not? You look at someone like Rip Van Winkle and laugh. "It's so simple! How come he doesn't get it? Where has he been?"

If you were born earlier than 1980, you may feel a bit like Rip himself, waking up to a world you don't recognize. You saw it happen right before your eyes, yet you may still not be totally comfortable with the idea of a phone that is also your calendar, address book, photo album, reference library, bank machine, and hi-def wireless video studio. You update your Facebook page, but you may not be sure why it matters, or if you're doing it right. Yet you know that this is the way the world is going. You feel that you have no choice but to get on board, and fast.

When massive change is thrust upon us and our businesses, our first question is likely to be, "what should I **do** about this?" The world tells you, "you need a website." So you get one up and running. Quickly, though, you discover that having a website is not enough; you need a Facebook page, a Twitter account, a blog, and an e-mail list. You're told that traditional media (radio, TV, newspapers) are all "dead or dying." Instead of buying conventional advertising, you are urged to spend your budget on pay-per-click and social media campaigns.

You're not sure that any of this advice is right, but you don't feel completely comfortable in this brave new world, and you feel you have no choice. Do it—or get left behind. To make all of this even more threatening and complicated, government regulations, industry consolidation, increasing competition, and the relentless compression of time and attention leave many of us running desperately to catch up. We know we can't work all the time, but we feel like we have to.

When change happens, we human beings most always default to action. But we would like to propose another way to remain successful while dealing with ever-present change. As Dr. Wayne Dyer famously said: "I am a human being, not a human doing."

This book invites you to shift your focus from "doing" to "being." That's because one thing has not changed: the importance of human presence. And presence is first and foremost a matter of "being." This book is all about that.

Initiating Change

In this environment of accelerating change, the archetypes of humanity remain constant. Among them are those who want to make a difference: A host of healthcare professionals: integrative and wellness practitioners, nurses, pharmacists, traditional healers, caregivers, mental health counselors. A phalanx of the public-minded: lawyers, advocates, social workers, service professionals, and government employees who refuse to lose sight of the people they serve. An army of altruists: those whose lives are wrapped up in the charities they head, the campaigns they drive, and the causes they fight for. Those who arm themselves not only with the tools of their trade but with idealism and a passion for helping others. These people have skills they wish to offer to the world, a message they believe in, and practices or businesses that are worth growing.

We bet there's a good chance that—on your best days, at least—you proudly see yourself as marching within these ranks. We wrote this book to amplify your message, to develop your presentation skills, and to help you grow your business.

Enhancing Your Presence

We began conducting our *Enhance Your Presence Training™ (EYP)* in-person courses in 2015, but the content and interactive exercises were shaped by our combined 1,000 presentations over the last 35 years—most of them oriented around personal growth, health and productivity, resilience, self-expression, leadership, and change and stress management. Early on, we set the ground rule that we would create a PowerPoint-free zone and focus entirely on providing our training as a series of small-group and individual exercises augmented by video coaching and counseling.

To date, most of our workshop attendees have been healthcare professionals. In some ways, this is a result of Mark's renown in this field. But it is also because we believe the healthcare field is the perfect place to catalyze a conversation on presence. Why?

For one thing, in the field of healthcare, there is purity to the relationship between patient and practitioner. Even the most hardened cynic, who bewails the commercialized state of healthcare in this country, recognizes the nobility of the calling of the medical profession. The best healthcare professionals operate from a deep sense of purpose. They have spent years learning the art and science of their discipline. They operate ethically and always have the best intentions for their patients. We believe this kind of customer-centered dedication distinguishes the leading firms in *every* field. And we think that's why our work—originally designed for healthcare practitioners—has found such broad appeal.

What would the world be like if every product and service were created and delivered with the kind of attention and intention that you expect from the best doctor?

In a world where a single bad Yelp review can severely damage a business, there is no room for anything less than the best.

To make our insights as accessible as possible to the broadest audience, this book will draw examples from many fields, and from many leaders, many of whom have little to no association with healthcare. Regardless of your professional field, we are confident you will find illustrations and insights that can be applied to your unique situation.

In today's promotion-centered world, success requires every one of us to do a better job communicating our unique value proposition in person, online, and on camera. In this book, we will discuss in-person presence, as well as presence that is conveyed over various media. We believe that the ability to create and use media effectively is an essential and basic skill in today's business world. And yet, it is a skill that is not taught as part of any professional curriculum.

Media-literacy is the new literacy. We recognize that literacy is the foundation for communication, for understanding, for interpretation and creation. If you cannot read, you are shut out from humanity's collective conversation. If you cannot write, you are unable to contribute to that conversation. Today, that global conversation is carried forward in podcasts, websites, and viral videos. How to record an audio, or appear on camera, is now a skill as essential as writing an essay.

In fact, it is the same skill, differently employed. When writing an essay, you select a point of view and a narrative voice that defines who is speaking. You create a beginning, middle, and end. This is how you also create a script for a video. Except that the video involves performance as well, the skill by which you bring your words to life on the screen in front of a camera.

Media literacy, which we sometimes call "mediacy," is as essential as reading and writing. As CEO of your brand, you don't need to do it—but you do need to know how it's done, and how to manage it so that it's done well.

Our Promise to You

As we begin each *EYP* workshop, we offer a list of promises to our participants backed by an unconditional tuition refund guarantee. The terms of our pledge are simple: Complete the workshop. If you feel we have not delivered to your satisfaction on each promise, simply tell us and we will give you an immediate refund, no questions asked. Here are the promises: In this program you will:

1. Move beyond trying to "act natural" to actually being comfortable and authentic.
2. Expand your natural ability to serve, guide, and influence.
3. Become more influential so that your messages are received favorably and acted upon.
4. Tap into your passion and use this energy to capture and hold the attention of your audience.
5. Discover your own natural charisma. As a result, your presentations are credible, authentic, and authoritative.
6. Have fun with yourself and others.
7. Gain the power to recognize and tailor your message to the different learning styles of others.

We have seen how the concepts embodied in this book have changed the perspective of our workshop participants. They come away from our time together with two things: a new insight into what messages they should create and send; and a new sense of confidence that sending those messages will actually make a difference—both for them and for the recipients.

You may never get to attend one of our live events. But we hope the ideas, concepts, tips, and techniques in the pages ahead will serve you as you serve humanity.

Chapter 1

The Roots of Presence

"My presence speaks volumes before I say a word."
— Mos Def, American Hip Hop Artist

What is Presence?

Presence is an intentionally generated state of human consciousness, arising from mindful attentiveness to one's own self and another human being.

People to People is Presence, Anything Else is Not

It's not easy to define presence without invoking the word "present." A common definition, in addition to the two above, states that presence is the "quality of being present." The key word in this sentence, however, is not "present"—it is "being."

We are talking about much more than mere existence. If we are in a room with a person who is asleep, we may feel that we are present, but we are pretty sure they are not—at least not in a way that is useful. We need them to "wake up and BE present." But being conscious is not the same as being present. To say it a different way: "We need them to wake up and *cause their presence to be.*"

15

Presence is a caused phenomenon. It is a state that we can turn on or turn off at will. There is nothing accidental about it. At the heart of *Enhance Your Presence* are two ideas, each of which involves active, moment-to-moment creation or causing: **intention** and **attention.**

When I am causing my presence to be of service to others, I give up outside concerns and distractions. I intentionally direct my focus to you, now, in this moment. I generate the **intention** to pay **attention** to you. You feel I am "with you." You may even feel I am here "for you."

Why is this so vitally important? Our media-saturated society has placed a supremely high value on attention. To attract a customer, we must first get their attention. And the best way to gain attention is to first pay attention.

The task of enhancing presence starts with us. It begins when we notice that there is a difference between daydreaming and focused listening. The mind loves to wander. We must heighten our awareness of this because:

> *Presence is a generated phenomenon. The minute you stop generating it, it vanishes.*

Businesses Have Presence . . . but Often, Not Enough!

Perhaps every instance of poor customer service is actually rooted in a palpable lack of presence. Either the business has failed to be present itself—say, when you spend an hour on hold—or the business has failed to intentionally direct its focus on you, taking you for granted and refusing to develop personal interactions with you. "They treated me like I wasn't even there," is a common refrain one hears from disgruntled customers.

It is Business 101 that you should pay attention to your customers throughout the business relationship. But if you look at your interactions with your customers through the lens of presence, it will be clearer how to strengthen this relationship. Businesses that survive and thrive are those that generate and sustain among customers the strong feeling that the business is present in every interaction, throughout the entire cycle of buying and consuming products and services.

This is why we say:

"To grow your business, you must first enhance your presence."

Presence Involves a Value Exchange

What determines a "customer" may not be an immediate exchange of money, as in a purchase. It's the exchange of *anything of value* that makes someone else's life better, whether it's obvious in the moment—or has eventual value later.

"Time is money." Likewise, attention is currency. If we ask someone for money—or any of its proxies like time, attention, belief, followership, endorsement, influence, even Facebook likes, etc.—that person is properly (if not explicitly) defined as our customer, client, patron, follower, believer, endorser, adherent, partner, or associate. They have something we want. And we're willing to give up something to get it. That's a value exchange. There are a few other ingredients in the giving-getting exchange. These include:

Likeability. When people like us, they are more likely to buy from us. So giving a presentation to people who could like us is actually part of the "customer development" or selling cycle. (In healthcare, we know that patients are less likely to sue doctors they like.)

Social proof. This happens when people tell others that they like us and benefit from what we do. Those recommendations influence more people to follow us. Followers can become buyers, clients, partners, or patrons. This is why testimonials and referrals are paramount for growing your business.

Authority. At a certain point, our service accumulates a certain number of satisfied customers who are recommending us to their friends and in public forums. Social proof reaches a tipping point and becomes authority. That's the stage at which it seems like "everyone agrees" that our service is valuable. Similarly, authority can arise from a well-respected public figure endorsing us, either by rendering an expert opinion, or responding to many instances of social proof.

Persuasion. For people who think, "selling is bad," this ingredient is an unwelcome one. But it's inescapable. Everyone we speak to is a customer or potential customer. Some of them actually buy from us. But even if they don't—they can like us, follow us, and recommend us to others.

Presence is Not Fake; Presence is Not Slick

There is a difference between likeability and persuasion, and manipulation. So let us include, in this conversation about presence, a negative definition: Presence is not manipulative. It is not dishonest. It is not inauthentic.

When we define presence as simply "being here now," this lesson is obvious. But when we begin to explore the link between "being present" and "presentation," this message is often lost or discarded.

In our workshops, one of the most common fears we hear from participants is that they are afraid of appearing too polished, too "slick." In other words, they are afraid of appearing not genuine. People fear that their audience will view them as inauthentic, but more than that, they fear having to hide part of their personality simply to present their ideas.

This fear comes from the expectation that a good presenter must conform to the mold of the charming car salesman, the charismatic visionary, the street preacher. There is an expectation that shy or introverted people must pretend to be something they are not, when they are presenting.

We disagree. Enhancing your presence does not require you to plaster on a fake smile or to adopt a second personality. Instead, enhancing your presence requires that you tap into your authentic self, and that you communicate your passion to others.

Google is constantly tweaking its search engine algorithm to better serve its users. One of their biggest changes happened only recently: Google has revealed that its search engine will reward sites with "authority," placing them higher in the rankings. Since this announcement, websites the world over have scrambled to position themselves as leaders and experts, thinking these terms connote authority.

But expertise is not the only constituent element of authority. Instead, *author*-ity arises from *author*-ship. Authors are people who create unique content—content that is useful and that is not derivative. It is content attributable to an author—a person.

This type of content stands in stark contrast to the babble-speak of legalese or the vague clichés of hive-mind corporate writing. When you visit the webpage of a corporation, you may find content about its experts and leaders, but you may not find any content authored by them.

Authority and authenticity are, of course, related concepts. One has only to look at their shared Greek etymology, their linked linguistic DNA, to see that this is true. Their common root, *autos*, means "self." Authenticity and authorship both require that you be unapologetically yourself, that you not mimic anyone.

When you present, you are providing unique and useful content to your audience. Even if this presentation is on publicly available information, your analysis and conclusions are your own. You are an authority on everything you present, not because you are a leader in the field or an expert on the subject (although you very well may be) but because you have provided something original to your audience.

Presence is Person-to-Person

Ursula K. Le Guin, the American novelist, is perhaps most famous for her 1974 book *The Dispossessed*. In it, an alien scientist visits the Earth-like world from which his people originally came. The inhabitants who receive him are shocked to learn that his people have successfully created a society that has no government, no war, no racism or sexism, and no inequality. One woman confronts the scientist, exclaiming that "The law of evolution is that the strongest survives!" To this, the scientist replies, "Yes, and the strongest, in the existence of any social species, are those who are most social."

Indeed, the animal skills of size, speed, and strength are not the same skills that humans have used to become the dominant species on the planet. One of our key skills is our ability to work in groups, to interact and empathize with one another, to share information and knowledge with those around us. As we have changed—from hunter-gatherers with sticks and stones, to urban professionals with lattes and laptops—these skills remain vital to success.

Today, we can use our computers and smartphones to remotely and instantly access 24/7 news, customer service hotlines, our e-mail, our work, and on-the-go entertainment. Yet despite all this—or perhaps because of all this—we still chafe when companies deliver impersonal customer service. We still fly halfway across the country to meet friends for special occasions. We still feel the meaning behind the words "I'll be home for the holidays." We still have office buildings where co-workers physically congregate, sometimes commuting for hours.

In fact, our emphasis on in-person professional interactions may be increasing. For example, marketing group Weber Shandwick, along with the Institute for Public Relations, researched the attitudes millennials take towards their work. Being the most e-connected generation of all time, it would be natural to expect that they would value online communication over in-person interaction. The research results, however, indicate the exact opposite. For instance, 34% of millennials believe that physically meeting with co-workers outside of work is important for building a positive work reputation. Only 15% of baby boomers and 14% of Gen Xers felt similarly.[1]

In short, we still recognize the value of social presence. We still crave the feeling of a personal connectivity that cannot be captured through e-mail attachments. We still intuitively understand the importance of authentic and personalized communication.

So, with this background in mind, let us make one of our biggest assertions in this book on the power of enhancing your presence.

Presence occurs in person-to-person interactions. In every other type of interaction, that presence is diluted.

The Mediated Presence

We have used the word "media" for so long to refer to our various instruments of communication—video, newspaper, radio, and so on—that we may forget the original meaning of the word. Media, a word borrowed directly from Latin, simply means "middle." Our communication medium is the instrument that stands in the middle, between the message sender and message receiver.

Today, businesses and professionals use media—be it a website, a Twitter account, LinkedIn, or Facebook—to deliver their message, a message that they could not transmit as broadly person-to-person. A mediated presence offers opportunities, but also challenges. We will explore how to ensure that your presence, when mediated, is not diluted to the point where people feel that you are divorced from your message.

Let us suggest something that may seem counter-intuitive: You cannot be present later. Presence is a function of time. If I am present with you, that is something that can only occur *now*, in the moment.

And this is one of the great flaws of equating "social media presence" with actual presence. A series of back-and-forth tweets, a frozen LinkedIn picture, a Facebook message to which you eventually respond . . . This is indirect communication, over time, through a medium. It is a form of presence, but one that is significantly diluted.

Much of the power of Facebook comes from the fact that we are seeing posts from people we know. We have positive, even fond memories of times we were together. When we see a newly posted picture of our friends happy in their new home with their cute new dog, we smile at much more than just the picture and the words. Human beings remember. This is why our interactions with customers must always be memorable and positive, so that when they encounter us online, they have a positive reaction.

Most Presence is Mediated

Let's imagine a thought experiment: that time machine you've been working on in your garage is finally completed, and you jump back in time to watch the first mass-produced computer being created. Jump in the time machine again, and go back to the first mass-produced typewriter. Jump in the time machine again, and go farther back, to the invention of the printing press.

Each time you go back, to a world on the brink of a massive shift in the way we communicate, imagine yourself walking the streets, talking to the people who have first tried the typewriter, or the computer. Ignore the people who love the new technology, the ones who eagerly embrace it. Instead, talk to the people who hate it, who distrust it, who worry that some of the poetry has gone out of the world with this new technological development.

Every development in communication, from the dawn of time, has removed the communicator from the people he or she is communicating with. That is, of course, the point: an author can reach people continents away with her new book; a skilled orator can share his message beyond those within earshot via podcast. Today, we send e-mails to people half the world away, and they receive the message almost instantaneously. But, regardless of the incredible benefits this has provided, the prevailing trend of communication technology has been to create more and more media that separate us from our audience.

Socrates, the ancient philosopher, wrote down not a single word of his lessons. The world knows of his contributions only because of the diligent writings of his apprentice, Plato. Socrates distrusted the written word. If men learn to read and write, he taught,

> "...it will implant forgetfulness in their souls; they will cease to exercise memory because they [will] rely on that which is written, calling things to remembrance no longer from within themselves, but by means of external marks. What you have discovered is a recipe not for memory, but for reminder. And it is no true wisdom that you offer your disciples, but only its semblance, for by telling them of many things without teaching them you will make them seem to know much, while for the most part they know nothing, and as men filled, not with wisdom, but with the conceit of wisdom, they will be a burden to their fellows."[2]

Much of this quote has to do with memory versus memorization, but within this quote is also the idea that personal, unmediated conversation is a more effective way to communicate an idea than writing.

Socrates' thesis—that new advances in communication technology may in fact distance us from the message—lives on, even today. In a 2014 study, for example, psychological scientists analyzed two groups: students who took notes by hand, and students who took notes by computer. The students who took notes by hand performed better at remembering the ideas of the lecture than the students who took notes via computer; in some cases, significantly better.[3] A logical inference is that the computer note-takers, relying on an easier medium for verbatim transcription, were not engaging with the material to the same extent as their handwriting brethren.

When our message is mediated, our presence is diluted. A sales pitch made in person is usually more effective than a pitch made over the phone. An in-person meeting with a doctor is far more valued by a patient than an online diagnosis. Handwritten letters are treasured by friends and family; e-mails never leave the computer.

One challenge, then, is to figure out how to convey as much presence as we can, over these media. Another challenge is to identify which media dilute our presence less than others, and craft strategies for enhancing our presence accordingly.

Show Your Face: Enhance Your Presence Using Video

Video is a medium in which the speaker's presence is less diluted than it is in many other formats. The capacity for the presenter to be both seen and heard allows for much more of his or her personality to come through to the audience. Video allows not only for the delivery of the message, but also for the audience to put a face to the message.

The importance of the face cannot be overstated. When someone wants to sum up their negative experience with a large company—when they have reached out for help with a problem and they have found no one present—they will often complain about a "faceless corporation." This turn of phrase is telling. It would be crazy to complain about a "bodyless corporation." We know that corporations have a physical existence—buildings, stores—and that they are staffed with hundreds or thousands of people who inhabit physical bodies. But when we say a "faceless corporation," everyone understands what we mean: there is no meaningful interaction, no genuine human being on the other end of the phone or e-mail link who feels invested in helping you. And, as a short-hand for all this, we say that they are "faceless."

Video allows you to present your face to your audience. Immediately, you become a living, breathing human being, with the capacity for empathy and connection.

With video, your persona is also magnified by the addition of voice. You can influence and reach others with your vocal timbre, tone, pacing, phrasing, and emphasis. Your verbal delivery alone can move people to a host of emotions. The power of the spoken word is celebrated in this excerpt from "Lift Off," a poem that student Donovan Livingston recited to fellow students at the Harvard Graduate School of Education 2016 commencement:[4]

> I was in the seventh grade when Ms. Parker told me,
> "Donovan, we can put your excess energy to good use!"
> And she introduced me to the sound of my own voice.
> She gave me a stage. A platform.
> She told me that our stories are ladders
> That make it easier for us to touch the stars.
> So climb and grab them.
> Keep climbing. Grab them.
> Spill your emotions in the big dipper
> and pour out your soul.
> Light up the world with your luminous allure.

The speech itself is being hailed as one of the greatest commencement speeches ever. And while you can certainly feel the power of the words themselves, you will also see the reflected passion in Livingston as he recites the words, captured on video and now being viewed by millions: (http://www.gse.harvard.edu/news/16/05/lift)

We all know the phenomenon of the viral video: the new video clip, like Livingston's, that suddenly explodes to the point where it seems like everyone has seen it. When a video—pictures and sound—goes viral, it has succeeded because it has generated an emotion in the viewer. That emotion does not need to be a forceful one: amusement is an emotion, and often the right emotion to feel when we're watching, say, the newest video of a dancing pig. What these viral videos share is that they evoke an emotional response in us. They capture—and keep—our attention because they cause us to wonder, laugh, be inspired, feel angry, become curious, or take action.

This is the power of video. Perhaps the best examples are TED Talks. These videos and their unique alchemical formula of biographical confessional and worldly insight have launched movements and changed lives. Take the case of Brené Brown, PhD, a research professor at the University of Houston Graduate College of Social Work, whose TED talk on "The Power of Vulnerability" has been viewed more than 25 million times. Brown shares personal and powerful stories about the relationship between vulnerability, empathy, and authenticity. On video, she strikes a universal chord with the viewer, compelling our engagement.

Attendees in our *Enhance Your Presence* workshops have their own inspiring stories and unique experiences. Not infrequently, they ask us, "How can I get a TED Talk?" When we hear this question, we understand that they're not asking us for help submitting their application to TED. Instead, they are asking about presence. How can they project their presence across the medium of video to the greatest effect? How can they ensure that their story will have the same power and impact as the great TED Talks that they have seen? How can they catch lightning in a bottle? How can they go viral?

We always respond to these questions in the same way:

Presence requires patience and practice.

Today, we are distracted and led astray by the successes of reality TV. We see people achieve instant success simply for being on-screen. We forget that we are not seeing these people as they are, but as an image curated by a team of editors and videographers. Increasingly, we are trained by this glut of reality television to think that a successful video presence requires nothing more than a camera and the blinking red light to show that it is recording.

But the more steadfast path to success involves doing the work to discover who you are, what you believe in, and how you will take your message to the world. What brings our clients to enroll in our *Enhance Your Presence* training program is the realization that there is a gap between their current abilities and their envisioned potential. This gap is the source of the pervasive fear surrounding speaking in public or appearing on video. "I'm not good enough, so rather than risk it, I will abstain."

We know where you're coming from because we have been there. But we also believe that "being charismatic" is not a divinely conferred attribute given to only a few. We believe it is an ability anyone can acquire if they are willing to learn and practice some defined skills. That's what this book, and our work, are ultimately about: achieving an enhanced presence in person, on camera, and online.

Now, video doesn't solve all problems. We cannot forget that even in video, presence is still diluted. There is no substitute for personal, in-the-flesh presence. It's a truth known by every music or sports fan. The event is always better live. It is why we say to our friends, "You should've been there," instead of saying "You can watch it on video. It'll be the same." There is an intangible but real aspect to one's presence in person, something that no video can convey.

The perfect illustration of the difference between personal presence and in-video presence comes from Man's Best Friend. Mark's household, like over a third of all American households, is a dog-owning home. Two dogs, to be precise. His wife engages in a strange ritual every time she travels. She will call home using a video device (like FaceTime or Skype), and after she talks to the family she'll ask to see the dogs. And when the two dogs hear her voice, and see her face on the screen . . . they don't respond. They may occasionally glance at the phone or perk their ears up, but overall their reaction is distinctly underwhelming.

Now, despite what some believe, dogs are capable of viewing two-dimensional videos, just as humans are. A dog's visual skills are so developed that they can pick out the faces of other dogs on video screens using visual clues alone.[5] Mark's wife's image and voice come through loud and clear; Mark is certainly able to recognize her. But to the dogs, because her scent is not present, she is *not there*.

The power and connection of in-person presence has no equal. Despite the reach of video, it cannot make up for a lack of personal presence. A truth so simple, a dog can understand it.

The Flip Side of Presence: Reception

We have already talked about the attention that the presenter must pay to the audience: a good presenter has the intention to pay attention to the other person.

Because communication is a two-way street, both the presenter and the audience must be attentive to the other for any message to be communicated. A transmitting radio does no good if there is no reception on the other side.

If presence is the transmission of a signal, the audience's attention is the reception of that signal. In a conversation, the speaker *must* be present, and the listener *should* be attentive. Notice the distinction: a presenter *owes* her audience her attention. But the audience doesn't owe the presenter anything; while it would be considerate if the audience gave the presenter their undivided attention, that consideration is far from assured.

Audience attention is becoming an ever-scarcer commodity. This is something we know intuitively: our phones are constantly beeping, the television screen is constantly flickering, and "clickbait" websites are constantly stealing our attention away. Our ability to focus on one thing for a sustained period is slipping away from us.

Our intuition about this is backed by research. The Microsoft Corporation released the results of a study last year, showing that our average attention span has dropped precipitously since the year 2000, from a twelve-second attention span to today's new total: an eight-second attention span. Mothers used to criticize their children by saying that they had "the attention span of a goldfish." But at a nine-second attention span, the goldfish is now more attentive than we are.[6]

When we speak, we are competing for access to a contested and limited resource: the attention span of our audience. As any good economist will tell you, when supply of a commodity goes down, the value goes up. With attention in ever-shorter supply, it has become an ever-more valuable commodity.

Everyone is in the Attention Business

One of America's most famous marketing gurus, Theodore Levitt, had a story he told in his legendary 1960 article "Marketing Myopia," a story that still circulates today amongst business leaders. It is a story about railroads. Or, more accurately, it is a story about railroad companies.

In the nineteenth century, railroad magnates were captains of industry. Railroad families like the Vanderbilts and the Stanfords were a titanic force in the American economy. But by 1960, railroads were a shadow of the industry they once were. Technology passed them by, and, despite a century-long head start, railroad companies were unable to stop their decline.

Why did railroad companies fail so spectacularly? Levitt offers the answer: "The railroads are in trouble today not because that need was filled by others (cars, trucks, airplanes, and even telephones) but because it was *not* filled by the railroads themselves. They let others take customers away from them because they assumed themselves to be in the railroad business rather than in the transportation business."

It was Levitt who showed the business world that every business must define itself by the needs of the customer that they seek to fulfill. It was due to Levitt that, when a company is soul-searching, its executives begin by asking, "What business are we in? What needs do we fulfill?"

Today, we find ourselves witnessing a similar collapse of an entire industry: traditional journalism. The death of old media is such an open secret that it has reached the point of cliché. Newspapers are going out of print, television news is scrambling for viewers, and venerable media institutions find themselves in cut-throat competition with year-old start-ups.

As two men who have both worked in media—Robert for more than 35 years—we are saddened by this change. But as businesspeople, we ask ourselves: what business are these companies in? Broadcasters see themselves as in the broadcasting business. They are not. Broadcasters are in the business of monetizing attention.

Here is another open secret:

Today, everyone is in the business of monetizing attention.

Every company is engaged in the struggle to grasp and maintain the attention of others, be they clients, customers, patients, potential partners, fans, or voters. To further develop this point, consider:

In a complex world, the job of every business is to get noticed, known and remembered.

Melding Mindfulness into Presence

It was Cambridge, Massachusetts, in the 1970s, and the swing of the counter-cultural revolution was perhaps only dimly felt at the world-famous Massachusetts Institute of Technology. But it was there that a young and brilliant PhD student introduced himself to a bald-headed Buddhist monk, setting the stage for our modern conception of mindfulness. The monk was Philip Kapleau, a former war crimes court reporter and a Zen missionary. The young PhD student was Jon Kabat-Zinn, the

32

man most responsible for popularizing the concept of "mindfulness" in America.

In 1979, Jon Kabat-Zinn founded the Stress Reduction Clinic at the University of Massachusetts Medical School, where he created and refined the concept of Mindfulness-Based Stress Reduction (MBSR). Drawing heavily from Buddhist concepts, but placing his course in a scientific context instead of a spiritual one, Kabat-Zinn began teaching the benefits of mindfulness, an awareness in the here and now. Kabat-Zinn is perhaps best known for his second book, *Wherever You Go, There You Are*, the national best-seller owned by hippies and high-powered CEOs alike.

Kabat-Zinn offers this definition for mindfulness: "Mindfulness means paying attention in a particular way, on purpose, in the present moment, non-judgmentally."

We underscore two ideas in the definition. The first is: "paying attention in a particular way, on purpose." This suggests that to be mindful is to pay attention for a *reason*. It's more than Zen-like "observation." There is an outcome in mind, even if it's simply honoring another human being.

We also highlight the concept of paying attention non-judgmentally. In his best-seller *Seven Habits of Highly Effective People*, Stephen Covey tells us to "seek first to understand rather than to be understood." Unless we adopt this as an intentional practice, Covey warns, "You may ignore the other person completely, pretend that you're listening, selectively hear only certain parts of the conversation or attentively focus on only the words being said, but miss the meaning entirely. So why does this happen? Because most people listen with the intent to reply, not to understand."

Robert's father, a board-certified general surgeon, related this story: A patient came in complaining that his stomach hurt. Dr. Hughes said: "Show me where it hurts." The patient indicated the area around his belt line. Dr. Hughes knew instantly that the stomach couldn't be the problem because the stomach is located well above the navel. Even so, Dr. Hughes continued: "How long has your stomach been hurting?"

This story demonstrates the power of listening while purposefully suspending the need to reply, argue, or instruct. There was simply no need to correct the patient's mistaken notions about human anatomy. That would have demonstrated the doctor's medical knowledge, but would not have improved the patient's condition even a little. Aristotle said, "It is the mark of an educated mind to be able to entertain a thought without accepting it." We say:

> *When you give up the debate in order to serve another, it is the mark of an open heart that manifests as enhanced presence.*

So if mindfulness is purposeful awareness and attention to the present moment, how does it differ from presence? After all, this book is called *Enhance Your Presence*, not "Enhance Your Mindfulness." Mindfulness and presence are linked concepts, but they are not the same. We suggest that, in our definition of presence, it differs from mindfulness primarily in its degree of activity and intention.

When you are mindful, it is enough to be in the moment. But presence, that ability we seek to enhance, gives mindfulness direction and purpose. With presence, you are not merely mindful of others, but you are invested in their worth, their work and its purpose. Mindfulness calls for us to listen to others without judgment or distraction. Presence requires not only that we listen to others, but that we also hold the mental resolution to assist them in their mission. Mindfulness allows us to say to others, "I am with you, in this moment." But it is presence that enables us to say, "I am *for* you, in this moment."

> *Presence is the combination of mindfulness and intention. Mindfulness grounds you in the moment, but intention allows you to set the path to move forward.*

It is this aspect of presence that lends itself to the legends we hear about particularly charismatic people. You know the lines: "When she talks to me, I feel like I'm the only one in the room." "He looked at me, and you could tell that he really saw me." This is the manifestation of presence: When you are present, you connect to the other person. They can tell that you hear their story. You may not agree with them, but you put that aside for the chance to step into their shoes and sample their reality. That simple act does a lot to get them on your side. People who are charismatic do this often and effortlessly.

What is Charisma?

Is it a rare gift, given randomly to only a lucky few? Is it an accident of birth, or bloodline? Is it the byproduct of an elite education? Is it conferred by money, looks, or native talent? Is it some combination of all of those? The dictionary definition says "charisma" is:

1. compelling attractiveness or charm that can inspire devotion in others;
2. a divinely conferred power or talent.[7]

The Greek root of the word means "favor" or "gift." Beginning in 1640, the word was used in mostly Christian contexts, referring to a divinely bestowed gift given to an individual by the Holy Spirit to benefit the Church. In 1922, that changed when the German sociologist Max Weber used the word in a secular context for the first time. His definition included the idea that charisma is rare and springs from a supernatural origin.

> "The term 'charisma' will be applied to a certain quality of an individual personality by virtue of which he is considered extraordinary and treated as endowed with supernatural, superhuman, or at least specifically exceptional powers or qualities. These are such as are not accessible to the ordinary person, but are regarded as of divine origin or as exemplary."[8]

Let's explore the notion of charisma as a divine gift vs. a developed skill. The authors noticed that when we discuss charisma among ourselves, we are biased in favor of people around whom there is broad agreement on three points:

1. They're "good people."
2. They're widely admired.
3. They've made a genuine difference in the world.

But we have to remind ourselves that charisma is not just for the "good guys" of history. If charisma is the ability to foster devotion and followership, certainly Osama Bin Laden, Adolf Hitler, Fidel Castro, cult leader Jim Jones, and Charles Manson all belong on a list of the charismatic. Their charisma arises from their extreme views powered by ego and willpower.

We might agree that certain athletes, rock stars, politicians, and actors are charismatic. People like David Beckham, Jennifer Lawrence, Muhammad Ali, Beyoncé, Steph Curry, Prince, and Marilyn Monroe. Their kind of charisma arises from one or more of these factors: talent, skill, appearance, performance, or the ability to create and project an image.

This is not about distinguishing sinners and saints. For our clients who want to spread their message, this is about putting your finger on precisely what it is that seemingly gifted leaders do to create an impact big enough to change the course of history. For purely practical reasons related to our topic of presence, when we discuss charisma, we focus on the kind of leaders who used their presence, and especially their speaking, to positively shape the direction of individual lives, movements, societies, and cultures.

Examples come readily to mind: Mother Teresa, John F. Kennedy, Martin Luther King Jr., Steve Jobs, and Mahatma Gandhi. When we think of them, we think mostly of the kind of people they were, what they said, and what they stood for on behalf of all people. With the exception of Mother Teresa, these people are not saints. They had human flaws, failures, character defects, and ethical missteps. But the fact remains: living their lives with the intent to impact all of us, their leadership resulted in massive and voluntary followership.

Perhaps the most accessible example of this kind of presence comes from former President Bill Clinton, a political figure who is simultaneously controversial yet, to some, enduringly popular. Clinton is well-remembered for the line "I feel your pain." In fact, some pundits believe that Bill Clinton clinched the presidency at a 1992 debate, when he and President Bush were asked a question about the national debt.[9] President Bush quickly got off on the wrong foot with his answer, and the audience member who asked the question repeatedly interrupted him to ask, "How can you help us if you don't know what we're feeling?" When then-Governor Clinton answered the question, he first asked, "How has it affected you again? You know people who lost their homes?" Then, he began his answer to the question this way:

"I've been governor of a small state for 12 years. I'll tell you how it's affected me. Every year, Congress and the President sign laws that make us do more things and give us less money to do it. I see middle-class people whose services have gone down while the wealthy have gotten tax cuts. When people lose their jobs, there is a good chance I know them by their name. If the factory closes, I know the people who ran it."

This was a quintessential "I feel your pain" answer. Clinton was not afraid to delve deeply into the questioner's experiences; then he demonstrated that he understood her situation because he himself had seen it and he clearly empathized. Unlike Bush, Clinton put himself squarely in the same boat with the questioner, before steering it along the course he had proposed. Months later, he was America's next President.

We re-tell this story not to make a political statement, but to demonstrate the constituent elements of presence, as demonstrated by a leader who has become world-famous for his personal charisma. Go back to the first part of Clinton's quote above ("How has it affected...") and count the number of times Clinton said "you" —two times in as many sentences. It is perhaps the mightiest of all the personal pronouns because it forges a connection. Clinton was being mindful. In the moment, he engaged with the questioner, enabling her to present her story without having it packaged into a political narrative. Then, in the second portion of his response, he used the word "us" several times. The only time he used the word "I" was to locate and position himself as an observer who sees and understands "your" problem. "I was a governor... I know people like you." He located himself in a place that made him a sympathetic witness. Then, with his answer, he demonstrated his empathy and understanding.

Major Presentation Tip:

> *Even when you are speaking in the largest room you can imagine, the word "you" connects you to each individual on a personal level. Make sure you're saying "you," "your," "yours," "we," and "us" far more often than "I," "me," and "mine." As words go, "you" is pure power. It works on the big stage as well as in the smallest, most intimate conversations.*

(AUTHOR'S NOTE: We put this in italics for one simple reason: we are unable to use blinking orange neon. This is really important! Use the magic of "you.")

Back to the charisma question: Divine gift? Or a skill to be developed?

We believe every human being is born with the potential to be charismatic. That potential is actually a talent—like art, music, or athletics. That much of it is God-given. Some people are born with so much talent that they are considered prodigies. But others, even those with less talent, can become competitive, sometimes even masterful, in this arena by combining their lesser gift of native talent with larger amounts of acquired knowledge, practice, and experience.

After we explain to our clients that it's possible to develop their charisma through knowledge and practice, we often follow up by asking: Why do you want to be charismatic? What doors does it unlock for you?

They tell us that being more charismatic would allow them to expand their personal power, increase their professional influence, help more people, and thereby improve their business results.

If charisma could be encapsulated in a checklist of mental habits, it might look like this:

1. **Treat everyone as if they are important**. We love the Hindu greeting "Namaste" which translates as "I bow to the divine in you." You don't have to say it, just live it always.

2. **Give the gift of a warm welcoming handshake.** Robert got to shake hands with blues guitar legend BB King. He remembers BB's warm, thick-callused fingers, his firm but gentle grip and his hearty "Hi, how are you?" His handshake said, "Welcome and thank you for loving my music."

3. **Keep your body relaxed, upright and open.** Stand tall but not stiff, weight slightly forward as if leading from your heart. Keep hands away from your face and mouth. Uncross arms and legs so you don't appear to be blocking the other person from reaching you. Speak with your hands to illustrate your words, even when not on stage. Posture and gesture communicate confidence.

4. **Remember names; notice faces, eye color, and other details**. Pay attention to your addressees' personality, background, and physical traits, and draw on them appropriately in conversation: "Brad, I liked the way you delivered that last line, especially the way you paused and looked around the room. It felt totally natural. Was it comfortable for you?" Incorporating personalized

details about the people you interact with communicates to them: "I see you, I notice you, I like you." Paul McCartney is world-famous for his music. But according to those who meet him face-to-face, it's an amazing experience because he knows that this is your personal "Beatle moment"—probably the only one you'll ever have—and he wants it to be even more memorable than you thought it ever could be. If Paul can give a gift of that magnitude, any of us can, too.

5. **Give compliments freely**. Make sure they are genuine and well-deserved. You never make yourself less by telling someone else how great they are.

6. **Speak slowly and clearly**. Choose your words as if they are a gift. Present your gift of words with the intention to contribute to others.

7. **Smile**. But not that fake "say cheese" smile. Instead, practice the Duchenne smile. It involves two sets of muscles: the "say cheese" muscles that lift the corners of the mouth, and the muscles that raise the cheeks and create crinkly crows feet around your eyes. This is the smile that looks real, because it is. It comes from the heart. Practice this in front of a mirror or on video so that you will know what it feels like.

There is Dynamic Tension in Every Living System

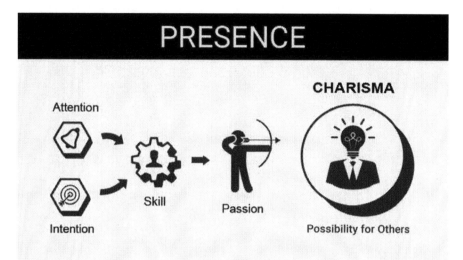

The visual above displays the model we have developed to describe the process of enhancing your presence. Unfortunately the two-dimensional aspect of circles, words and arrows fails to capture the dynamic tension in this system. It is this dynamic tension that provides the energy for presence.

There will always be tension between attention and intention. After all, how can you be grounded in the present moment, while at the same time having the intention to move forward onto a future path? Clinton's debate answer helps demonstrate the way to reconcile these two impulses: recognition that one cannot chart a way forward until and unless one truly understands where one is at the present moment—which includes understanding the other people around you. Wherever you go, there you are, indeed.

There are well-intentioned people in the world, many of whom can focus on others and pick up cues and clues from their environment. It is only through the application of skills that intention can be realized, and not just any kind of skills, but techniques executed with passion—grounded in an unshakeable belief that you are there to serve others with your message. You are there to light up a possibility in others. This is how you get "there" from "here" and close the gap that we previously described.

Looking at the model, you will see we link "charisma" with "possibility for others." This is the "I feel your pain" quality that is essential for charisma. Charismatic people connect their stories to the audience, not to themselves. The great orators of history always paint a picture in which their audience is present. Kennedy talked to the American people about going to the moon, and depicted it as an accomplishment for the American people, despite the fact that only a select few astronauts and engineers would actually be involved in the program. Steve Jobs' speeches did not center around the money that Apple was making; they centered instead about what Apple's new products meant for the average consumer. It's almost as if Jobs was saying: "I know you want to change the world. We just made a new tool that will help you do that. Let me show you how cool this is." It's the theme of every major Apple product introduction. People will engage with your presentation to the extent that your presentation engages with them.

Presence Shapes the Servant-Leadership Relationship

Presence is a form of servant-leadership. Your work is not about you. It is about *them*, the audience receiving your message. The clearer that is, the more enthusiastically your message will be received, and the more charismatic you will be.

This is not a sales trick. This is an essential underlying reality to what constitutes charisma. When you present yourself to others, you are giving others a basic glimpse of your personality. So what do you want other people to see in you?

An ancient and well-known Jewish religious leader, sage, and scholar, Hillel the Elder, poses the question that each of us struggles with. Hillel says:

"If I am not for myself, who will be for me? But if I am only for myself, who am I? If not now, when?" – Ethics of the Fathers, 1:14

There is no charisma to be gained from presenting only for yourself. Your presentation will rise and fall by the possibilities that it offers others: possibilities for the future, possibilities for change, possibilities for a new path. From this, charisma arises.

So there is no need for you to receive a charisma transplant. You can grow your own charisma, through practice, through experience, and through reflection on the message you want to convey. This is the formula for enhancing your presence and becoming naturally charismatic in the process:

Merge attention and intention with the skills of presentation and persuasion to passionately paint a possibility for others.

An Action Plan for Presence

At this point, you've most likely got the idea that presence is more than just showing up, even though showing up is a prerequisite. Just like an out-of-shape muscle, presence can be strengthened through skills acquisition and practice. Our seven skills chapters will help you get in shape.

However, unlike exercise, which is primarily about taking certain actions, enhancing your presence is a combination of introspection and action. We'll help you get clear on your strengths and weaknesses. If you suffer from the insecurities of presentation anxiety, you'll be able to nip those fears in the bud. We'll guide you through some exercises that tap into your passion to unleash your charisma. You'll learn techniques to tell compelling stories that unleash emotional responses in your audience. Perhaps more importantly, you'll re-orient your messages so that they are clearly more for others than about yourself. Finally, we hope to set you on a path to personal transformation with the confidence that your practice will ultimately result in mastery.

However, before we move on to the seven skills, let's take a moment to dispel any myths that developing presence is magical. Although magic does occur in those special moments when presenter and audience align minds and hearts, presence is rooted in science. To this science we will now turn.

Before you turn the page...

Download our free *Video Presence Accelerator*. In this training, we show you exactly how you can produce a series of short videos designed to project your presence and attract customers. No complicated tech! You can even use your cell phone or tablet. If you think video is "hard to do," you will be surprised.

It's completely free. You can get it here:

bit.do/changewell

Chapter 2

The Neuroscience of Presence

*"Human minds are more full of mysteries than any written book
and more changeable than the cloud shapes in the air."*
—Louisa May Alcott

Presence can't be faked. This is in part because presence has very real, very physiological components to it. These are phenomena that the bodies and brains of human beings have evolved to sniff out, process, and generate, often on a subconscious level.

Why are we so confident about this? Because it shows up in the lab, for one thing. The existence of these physical elements of presence has been demonstrated time and again by recent, robust scientific studies. In this chapter, we will spare you the sometimes inordinate detail in order to give you some actionable "key points."

We hope you will come back to this information repeatedly.

Bad Science Abounds

Not all communications advice is backed up by good science. For example, take this adage, which is routinely peddled at presentation workshops across the nation:

- 55% of communication comes from visual cues, such as your body language;
- 38% comes from auditory cues, such as your voice's inflection;
- and only 7% of communication comes from the actual content of your words.

The idea that 93% of all communication is nonverbal is a juicy counterintuitive. Unfortunately, it's also an incorrect one.

This myth is a wild extrapolation from a very modest 1967 study done by Albert Mehrabian, a Professor of Psychology at UCLA. This study did *not* involve a full, live presentation. Instead, Mehrabian had participants listen to a recording of a single word ("maybe") spoken in several different ways by three women, while the participants looked at photographs of women's faces. The participants were then asked to guess how much the speakers seemed to like their audience. [10]

Mehrabian found that study participants relied more heavily on the photographs than on other cues when making this assessment. On average, the importance of facial, vocal, and verbal variables to participants was .55, .38, and .07, respectively. What can we safely conclude from Mehrabian's work?

Key Point: Tone of voice, facial expressions, and body language all need to be coherent with the content.

A jerky, jumpy, overly nervous presentation of a somber subject would clearly not work. Instead, a presentation is more engaging when the speaker's moves and gestures are in tune with his content. And, you should never over-focus on delivery at the expense of content. Rather, carefully prepare the words of your presentation and the manner in which you give it.

What We Remember

What is the best way to get people to remember what you say? One axiom that's snuck its way into a number of recent communications books and blogs is that people remember:

- 10% of what they read;
- 20% of what they see;
- 30% of what they hear;
- 50% of what they see *and* hear; and
- 90% of what they do.

This seems very specific and very scientific. But when we attempted to actually find the research, we couldn't. Dr. Will Thalheimer, a learning and performance strategist who holds a doctorate in human learning and cognition, says that many blogs have misattributed this statistic to a concept developed in 1942 by Edgar Dale, known as the "Cone of Experience." This is shown as an illustration on the following page.

Dale places "verbal symbols" at the top of the cone, indicating that they are least effective in generating memory. At the bottom of the cone are "direct personal experiences." That makes sense, doesn't it? We are more likely to remember something we did rather than a word we read.

The most important thing to know about memory, says Thalheimer, is that it is *highly variable*. It is therefore very difficult to quantify memory without having a lot of context about the learning situation.

Dale's Cone of Experience, as adapted from Dale's book, Audio-Visual Methods in Teaching (1969)[11]

What an individual will remember from a presentation depends on many factors, ranging from the manner in which the information is presented, to how much prior knowledge the learner already has. This leads us to a second important idea:

Key Point: Make your presentation relevant to the audience and drive it home by using combinations of learning methods.

The particular combination you brew up will depend on the *context* of your talk. It will hinge on you having developed an understanding of who you're talking to so that you can present your content in ways that will personally engage them. That's because human memory has been shown to work best when it's being fed information that's *relevant* to the listener.[12] What does "relevant" mean in this context? Research suggests that the most "meaningful" content for our memories is:

> A) content in which the listener feels personally invested—what's being said will impact her in some way; and
>
> B) content that is connected in some way to the presentation's previous content. In other words, the presentation should create a self-contained story arc, each segment logically linked to what precedes and follows it.[13]

Skillful blending of these two types of content will allow you to harness presence and forge a genuine connection with your audience.

Meet the Wandering Mind

As we mentioned in Chapter 1, we are living in a world of increasingly short attention spans. Worse-than-a-goldfish attention spans.

Studies have shown that high levels of mind-wandering mean we're less likely to understand and remember information delivered in written materials and in lectures; less likely to put our working memory to use during challenging tasks; and less able to competently perform crucial everyday tasks, such as driving.[14]

But the picture isn't totally bleak. Mind wandering has been linked to greater creativity in solving cognitive puzzles and everyday social problems. It also boosts our mood during an unpleasant task. It may even improve our ability to consider and re-envision problems we will face in the future.[15]

Most psychologists concur that mind wandering is an inevitable part of human behavior.[16] In fact, it accounts for almost 50% of our waking life, according to a recent study by Harvard psychologists.[17] So the first thing to remember about your audience, as you prepare a talk, is that their minds *will* wander from time to time. The more important thing to know is that you can reduce that percentage by using techniques to keep your audience engaged.

Capturing and Keeping Attention

Attention is like a bucket of water. We have a finite amount of it. Each new stimulus dips in and takes a spoonful or two away, decreasing the store of it that remains to be doled out.[18] How can you ensure that you collect *as much of* the water from your listeners' attention buckets as possible? And that once you have that precious attention, how can you direct it towards the most important aspects of the presentation you're giving?

The term "attention" can actually refer to two distinct cognitive processes. These two types of attention may have developed at different points in human evolution, and for different purposes. **Transient attention** is involuntary and brief, referring to our reptile-brain responses to new stimuli. **Sustained attention** is more under our control, and can be deployed for much longer.

When the Microsoft Corporation study found that human attention span is now only eight seconds long, what it was referring to was transient attention. What triggers transient attention is change and novelty. We will say more about that later.

Key Point: Grab your listeners' attention in the first eight seconds of your presentation.

Be like the concert pianist. They came to hear you make music, not talk about the cab ride to the concert hall. After you are introduced, sit down, and PLAY! Start your presentation with something that gets attention.

The rest of your presentation will rely on your ability to maintain your listeners' sustained attention. Their long-term attention is easier to control—if you go about it correctly.

Key Point: Adults can sustain attention for about 20 minutes.

That's the conclusion of Dianne Dukette and David Cornish (a psychologist and physician, respectively). According to TED talk curator Chris Anderson, this is the thinking behind why each TED talk is limited to eighteen minutes.[19]

Dukette and Cornish also point out most of us have successfully sat through many a two-hour movie in our lives. That's because we can re-set our attention every 20 minutes or so, if the talk, movie or activity continues to engage us. Other researchers say the re-set interval is even shorter. One study collected data on students attending a lecture and concluded that audience attention and retention drops dramatically after *ten* minutes if there is no pause or serious shift in material and/or presentation style.[20] That brings us the next insight:

Key Point: Keep shifting your material so you re-set sustained attention.

Build your presentation so that it has distinct sections, punctuated by "soft breaks." These could take many forms:

- Move to a new topic or turn a major corner in terms of the presentation's content.

- Switch from talking to your audience to having audience members talk to one another.

- Change up your media. Move from speaking to playing a video clip; from a PowerPoint with the lights dimmed to a slide-less interlude with the lights on; from a talk to a physical demonstration with props; etc.

- Ask your listeners a question.

- Tell a story. (See Chapter 5 for more information on why you should tell at least one story in almost every presentation.) Or, if you've already been storytelling, switch narrative modes: share a statistic; make an argument; etc.

- Bring another speaker onstage to share the talk with you temporarily.

- Have your audience actually get up to take a break and stretch their legs.

Mixing it up this way will not only help your audience feel more engaged with your presentation in the moment. It will also help them remember what you've said after the presentation is over.

Using fMRI, a special imaging technique that measures changes in brain blood flow, participants were shown a series of images, most of which adhered to a predictable pattern. But when presented with an image that was new, or outside the pattern, the brains lit up. Researchers found that subjects were more likely to remember "oddball" images—photos that broke from the pattern.

Scans of the participants' brains revealed a potential reason for this. The substantia nigra/ventral tegmental area, also known as the "novelty center" of the brain, is connected to both the amygdala (the brain's emotional processing area) and the hippocampus (which controls our learning). So when we see something unexpected, the researchers hypothesized, our brain's "novelty center" could be triggering both an emotional response and a learning response. The novelty center is telling our brains, "this is new, probably important—remember it."[21]

Making Memory Matter

How much people pay attention during a presentation is directly linked to how much of that presentation they'll retain. But gaining an audience's attention is only part of the battle.

Key Point: Know and use the three different kinds of human memory.

They are divided roughly by the span of time each can accommodate:

- **Sensory memory** holds basic auditory and visual input for less than two seconds.

- **Working memory** (sometimes called "short-term memory") is a holding-space where your mind processes what's currently going on, and hangs onto that information for about 15-30 seconds—if you don't actively strive to retain it. However, if you work to retain that information, or if that information is especially emotionally impactful or personally relevant to you, it can be moved into your long-term memory.

- **Long-term memory** lasts anywhere from 30 seconds to almost your entire life.[22]

For you as a speaker, the most important of these types of memory are the second and third. You must understand and respect the limits of your listeners' working memory capacities. By doing so, you will ensure that they can grasp and thread together the smaller parts of what you've been saying in a given segment of your presentation (working memory). And then, with the right approach, you can also make it likelier that you—and your content—will sink into your listeners' long-term memory and stay with them weeks, months, or even years after your talk ends.

Holding onto Memory

Cognitive scientist George Miller proposed that, at a given moment, your mind can only hold about **seven** discrete, unrelated pieces of information at once: single numerals; words; images; etc.[23]

This concept has gained such widespread acceptance in psychology that it's known as "Miller's Law." More recent research has suggested that when people are prevented from using memory strategies, the number of items they can retain may dip even lower to **three** items plus or minus one.[24]

An initial conclusion we can draw from this is that we must not overtax our listeners by cramming too much information into our presentations. They simply will not remember more than about seven new pieces of information from a single presentation. Understand the concept that the mind can retain only a limited number of "items," but be flexible about how you define an item.

Miller showed that by lumping items together into larger "chunks," we can remember seven *chunks* instead of seven individual items. A phone number might be thought of as ten separate items: 800-555-2413. *But*, we could also "chunk" this into the area code, the prefix, and the number.

You've seen and heard this in radio and TV commercials where ten digit phone numbers, like 800-555-7254 are spoken as "eight hundred... five-five-five... seventy-two, fifty four." Read it aloud giving weight to the pauses and you'll hear how a ten digit number gets "chunked" down into four items.

"Chunking" is a trick actors use to memorize a speech, word by word: they "chunk" the words into phrases, the phrases into sentences, and sentences into lengthy monologues. Here's how to apply this to your next talk:

> *Key Point: Plan your presentation as a series of nodes, clearly signposting each time you move to a new one.*

If you carefully arrange your presentation into coherent, self-contained "chunks," or nodes, a much higher percentage of your talk will stay with your listener. Don't make your audience do this work themselves (they simply may not have the cognitive capacity to do so). And within each node, be sensitive to the amount of information you're presenting within the 30-second span of working memory.

Where You Put Things Matters a Lot

A relevant concept from psychology is the **serial position effect**. This is the principle that when someone is presented with a series of chunks of information, she will most clearly remember the first and last chunks (all other things being equal). She is most likely to forget the middle chunks.

Key Point. What you say first and last is most likely to be remembered.

In addition to the amount of information that you deliver to your audience, the order in which you deliver it makes a big difference in how much they'll remember. This is true whether we're talking about working memory or long-term memory.

Communications professors at the University of Miami studied viewing habits during the Superbowl. The researchers found that watchers were able to recall the first set of ads with substantially better precision than ads from the middle or end of the game.[25] Another, similar study found that this "primacy effect" was especially pronounced when a longer period of time elapsed between commercial-viewing and testing.[26] And a study of 1,540 participants by cognitive neuroscientist Carmen Simon has revealed that, in general, people more clearly recall the slides from the first half of a slide presentation than from second half of the presentation.

What this means for you as a speaker is that you should consider very carefully how you begin your talk. The opening is the part of your presentation that your audience will most likely remember the best. This is another argument for avoiding preambles, logistics, and other non-vital content in your first few sentences of content. Instead, jump right into a grabbing anecdote, paradox, or one of the major takeaways of your talk. The primacy effect will help that key point become one of the main things your listeners remember about your speech.

Consider, too, that the conclusion of your presentation will also receive special weight in your audience's memory, though probably less so than your opening remarks. Simon's research suggests that it would be best to include the majority of your more important takeaways in the first half of your presentation.

Does this mean you should resign yourself to having the middle parts of your presentation be forgettable no matter what? Of course not. In fact, understanding sequence can help out here, too. Studying slide presentations, Carmen Simon found that, after 48 hours, subjects remembered an average of only four slides out of a twenty-slide deck.[27] At first glance, this seems like a distressingly low number—especially since many of us often give presentations to potential clients who will not be making a decision about our company or product until days or weeks after we talk to them. Fortunately, Simon's findings don't stop there. What she discovered leads us to the next key point:

Key Point. Shift your content or style every five slides.

Doing this increases memorability. Instead of a long, 20 slide presentation, build your deck in four chunks of five slides, with a shift in content or style every fifth slide. And make sure those fifth, tenth, fifteenth, etc. slides contain an important talking-point from your presentation. These, along with your opening and concluding slides, may well be one of the few slides your audience remembers when they are making relevant decisions weeks after your presentation. This next key point is obvious, but the reasons why may not be:

Key Point. Pictures are remembered better than words.

In addition to carefully considering the order of your slides, there's one more principle of neuroscience that can help make the middle (as well as the beginning and the end) of your talk more memorable. That principle, known as the **pictorial superiority effect**, tells us that we retain images better than we retain words. So, if we harness the power of pictures to help us tell our stories, we can make sure those stories stick with our audiences.

It turns out that the human memory for images is rather remarkable. In a classic study at the University of Rochester, scientists showed participants 2,560 images. Even after three full days elapsed, people were able to recall an average of over 90% of the images they'd seen.[28] And these numbers clearly trump our memories for words/text. Psychologists Allan Paivio and Kalman Csapo directly compared subjects' abilities to recall 72 images versus 72 nouns. After five minutes, participants remembered more than twice as many images as they did words.[29]

Why might this be? First off, our brains are naturally more attracted to images. In an experiment using an infrared device to track participants' eye movements as they looked at advertisements, researchers found that viewers' eyes tended to gravitate first towards images rather than text—even if the image was tiny.[30] So, if our visual intake includes both images and text, we *initially* pay more attention to the images. As we've already discussed, we are more likely to remember input that we're paying strong attention to.

On top of the differing amounts of attention that we pay to written versus pictorial stimuli, some psychologists believe that we also have a more efficient mechanism for forming *memories* of pictorial stimuli.[31] The **sensory semantic model** argues that images are easier for our brains to distinguish from one another at a perceptual level, and are therefore easier for us to imprint into our memories.

A related theory suggests that images may be especially memorable if they are accompanied by verbal information. Allan Paivio's **dual-coding theory** proposes that the human mind processes and recalls verbal and visual information along two different channels. If we are showed an image while the word for that image is spoken to us, our minds absorb that information along both the verbal and the visual channels. In contrast, when we merely hear a word, Paivio proposes, our brain is more likely to process that information along only the verbal channel.[32]

Attention Can't Be in Two Places at the Same Time

Paivio's theory also helps explain why it is quite difficult for our brains to listen to spoken words while we read words at the same time. Many proponents of the dual-coding model believe that our image and verbal processing channels each has limited bandwidth. So here's another obvious, but critically important key point:

Key Point. Do not read your slides to the audience.

This sounds counter intuitive. If the words they hear and the words you say are the same, isn't that a good thing? Turns out: it's a very bad thing indeed. Hearing and reading both fall into the verbal processing category, and thus hearing at the same time as we are reading can potentially overload our capacity for word-based input.[33] Indeed, research has suggested that listeners actually retain less information from a presentation when the presenter reads text off of a slide.[34]

This "redundancy principle" does not mean that *all* text on a slide will sabotage your audience's learning. Rather, it means that you should avoid replicating your speech verbatim on your slides.

Key Point. Remember, the mind is simple and easily confused.

Some speakers mistakenly believe that including wildly disparate elements gets attention. Not true. Scholars have found that presentations accompanied by graphics (and sound effects) unrelated to the content at hand decrease viewers' learning.[35]

Throughout this chapter, we've given you the tools to understand the cognitive abilities—and limits—of your audience. From memory to attention, your listeners' mental capacities should be among your top considerations as you prepare your presentation.

We've covered a lot. Knowing how your mind works, we think you could probably use a summary. So here it is in ten "key points." (Remember, this is a book—not a talk, so a printed list is OK.)

- Tone of voice, facial expressions, and body language all need to be coherent with the content.

- Make your presentation relevant to the audience and drive it home by using combinations of learning methods.

- Grab your listeners' attention in the first eight seconds of your presentation.

- Adults can sustain attention for about 20 minutes. Keep shifting your material so you re-set sustained attention.

- Know and use the three different kinds of human memory: sensory, working, and long-term.

- Plan your presentation as a series of nodes, five slides in each node, clearly signposting each time you move to a new one.

- What you say first and last is most likely to be remembered.

- Pictures are remembered better than words.

- Do not read your slides to the audience.

- Remember, the mind is simple and easily confused.

NEW TOPIC: When it comes to improving *your* capacities as a speaker and a doer, there's a lot of work that can be done before you even step on a stage for the first time. It's that work that we'll explore in the next chapter.

Chapter 3
Put "Being" First

"Be more than just what you do."
— George Foreman, discussing what he learned from the late
Muhammad Ali

People who attend our *Enhance Your Presence* trainings are fairly universal in their goals. They want to have three things: greater personal power, professional influence and business results. They are willing to spend a day or more with us so they can master the skills to have what they desire. Simple enough. It looks like this:

This thinking can lead to a feeling of desperation: "I want to **have** a big successful company. If I had that, I could **do** more to help customers. And if I did that I would **be** successful." In this paradigm, the path to success starts with "having" which results in "doing" which generates an outcome in the realm of "being.'" The problem, of course, is that mighty oaks spring from tiny acorns—and not vice versa. A formula that starts with the outcome as the first step is doomed to fail. We are saying something very different. We say:

> To grow your business, you must first enhance your presence.

We have distinguished presence as a generated "state of being." We've said that all it takes to generate presence is the intention to bring presence into being—that "being" comes first. And from generating a state of "being," the "doing" arises naturally, and can result in the outcome of us "having" what we want.

Apple computer did not start its business in 1976 with the iPhone. It started with an idea in a garage. There was something quite distinct in who Jobs and Wozniak were being.

So what was that state of mind?

In 1980, Steve Jobs declared that Apple's mission was: "To make a contribution to the world by making tools for the mind that advance humankind." There is no "having" stated or implied. There is no mention of generating wealth, maximizing financial returns, no promise to conquer competitors, create proprietary technology, or assert market superiority—just a simple statement of an intent to serve all people by "making tools for the mind." It's uncomplicated and humble yet grand and inspiring.

Apple's legendary attention to design and ease of use follows directly out of this declaration of being. A company that intends to serve all mankind would naturally make its products "cool" and devastatingly attractive so they will be desired by millions. That company would make them easy to use so they could actually *be* used, thereby changing the world. This mission statement calls on everyone under Apple's roof to pursue one outcome—"to advance humankind." It requires a distinct way of being that has penetrated the company to its core and powered Apple to become the world's most valuable brand.

If you do not have a mission statement for your company, perhaps the fastest path to creating one is to start with questions that generate presence: Who are we? Who do we seek to serve? Why are we doing this?

Participants who enter our workshop all have goals or outcomes they seek. In almost every case they think that achieving those goals requires something that they don't "have," which would enable them to "do" that which will result in achieving the goal.

We have observed something else: In *EYP* courses we create a loving, supportive environment in which our participants feel safe enough to try out some new presentation techniques. Many of them are quite convinced that they cannot do what we ask. In short order they discover that not only can they do it—but also they are unexpectedly good at it! This discovery causes a shift in who they are being. Out of this transformation—suddenly all kinds of things that were previously "impossible" now become not only possible but fun!

In an inconceivably short amount of time, we transform **have-do-be** into the following.

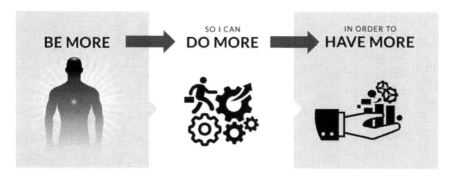

This shift in "being" opens the door to "doing" even things that were previously viewed as impossible. And out of that inspired kind of doing, wonderful "having" can occur.

Get the Sequence Right

Many Americans have closets and basements full of sports equipment. We thought that once we had that stuff we'd do more skiing, more tennis playing, more biking, more running. But our piles of dusty equipment are evidence that all of that stuff gets very little use. So what's the problem? The problem is that we're living life backwards. "Having" stuff does nothing to motivate us to use it.

On the other hand, if we're really motivated to be an athlete, lack of equipment won't stop us. The idea that we need to "have" before we "do" is an illusion.

Perhaps the most striking example is that of an African American boy growing up on a plantation in rural Louisiana. He had a music gene and a certain kind of music playing in his head, and he wanted to express that in a guitar. But he was too poor to afford a guitar. Being resourceful, he took a board from the side of the barn, stripped wire out of the window screen, and made himself a makeshift guitar. That person's name is Buddy Guy, one of the most legendary guitar players of all time. He didn't start out playing guitar with a Fender Stratocaster or a Gibson. He started out with a board and wire from a screen, because who he was *being* was a guitar player. Eventually he became a legend and inspired some of the greatest rock and rollers of all time.

Activities and possessions are both, by nature, transient things. They come; they go. "Being" is more permanent. Buddy Guy *was* a guitar player, even when he wasn't playing guitar. Our identity stays with us. It grants us permanence, like a phrase set in stone or a name written on a map.

Getting You on The MAP

We have always been partial to the map as a metaphor for permanence, presence, and identity. Some years ago, we were working with a public relations firm that, at the conclusion of their pitch, told us "You're in great hands. We're going to put you on the map." Obviously, they were speaking of their ability to have our product become well-known, and help us become important.

There's more to the expression. For just a moment, visualize a paper map and then find a spot that appeals to you. Now go ahead and stick an old-fashioned thumbtack in one spot. You are now on the map.

In fact, you have achieved a place, and a sense of permanence, that (unless you pull the pin), time cannot erase.

That's what you want to do with your presence.

You need to get on the MAP. And you can use three "being" skills to do so. You must be:

Memorable, Authentic and Persuasive.

Let's start with "memorable."

Being Memorable

We usually begin our workshops by asking attendees to think about the best presentation they have ever attended and who conducted it. Now, often years later, what do they remember and why? This recollection depends upon the attendee's occupation and interests, as well as experiences with spiritual teachers, scientists, authors, and more. However, in a few of our recent sessions, a number of people brought up Brené Brown's TED Talk, which we discussed earlier in the book.

Another of our attendees mentioned the impact that one of the United States' greatest academic leaders had made upon her. Here's what she said during the workshop:

"Many of you will not have heard of the name Nido Qubein. But some of you, especially in the fields of education, business management, or health, will have. I attend a lot of medical conferences, and I listen to a lot of presenters. But he was one of the best presenters I've ever seen, and it occurred at a chiropractic conference.

Firstly, Nido Qubein had presence. When you looked at him, you thought 'this guy is going to have something good to say. I can tell by the way he looks.' (We were intrigued enough to dig up a picture of Qubein, and we agree.)

And then he began to tell his story. Nido Qubein moved to the United States from Lebanon when he was seventeen years old; he had $50 in his pocket. Today, he is the CEO of the Great Harvest Bread Company, sits on the board of three other companies, and serves as the president of High Point University, in North Carolina.

Nido Qubein told us this story, a story of coming from nothing to being where he is today. When he told his story to us, you could tell that it wasn't to brag about his own self-worth. It was to demonstrate the path, to share his lessons with others. When he presented, you didn't have the feeling like you were being sold something. Instead, he was so genuine that you just wanted to hang on his every word, like what he would say next was so important that you just wanted to take it all in. The pacing and the timing of his speech left you in anticipation of what was going to come next."

The first thing that is so incredible about this story is the amount of detail the workshop attendee remembered. The powerful images—specific facts—burned into her brain.

We loved hearing this story, so we did a bit of research on Nido Qubein. We liked what we found.

As a recipient of the Horatio Alger award, Nido Qubein has many credentials on which he can rest his name. But when Qubein speaks to an audience, he does not derive his credibility from his titles or his credentials. Instead, he connects personally with his audience. He often begins his presentations by focusing the first few minutes on the experiences and the motivations of the audience itself. Going far beyond the pro forma "thank you for inviting me," he describes exactly what he appreciates about the audience, and what values he shares with them. When speaking to fellow entrepreneurs, he may open with a story about hustling to begin his first company, making sure to indicate his knowledge that this is an experience he shares with the audience. He may continue by saying, "You're my kind of people, and I'm glad to be with you this morning."

Qubein is the subject of a 2013 documentary on the Biography Channel. Throughout the inspirational story of his life, he has his share of verbal drops of wisdom, with sayings like:

- "It's not your circumstances that define your future, it's your choices. What you choose is what you get."
- "When you are passionate about something, and determined to make something happen, you just go about it with all the zest that you have."
- "If you are afraid of failure, you will never try success. And if you're afraid of failing, I'm not sure you deserve to succeed."

These sayings, as eloquent and clear as they are, only take on weight because Qubein can illustrate their truth by pointing to his own experiences. And this he does, bringing the audience with him through his life and walking with them to the destination he wants them to reach.

Of course, just as we asked others to share some of their favorite presentations with us, we should share our own favorite presenters with you. From these experiences, we can extract some lessons on the art of the presentation.

Mark's Most Memorable Presentation: Timothy Shriver

I had the privilege of attending a dinner event in Washington, D.C., where Timothy Shriver, the Chairman of Special Olympics, was scheduled to speak. Special Olympics serves over 4.5 million athletes and their families in 170 countries. From the very beginning of the event, you could tell where Shriver was within the room. He emanated the effortless Kennedy mystique and charisma. Everyone knew he would speak later that evening, and there were high expectations.

When it came time for speakers, Shriver told the story of his Aunt Rosemary, her life, and how she helped shape his life's mission to work with the disabled.

When he discussed the struggles of mental disability, the lessons learned, the inspiration that his Aunt Rosemary gave him, we forgot that "Aunt Rosemary" is Rose Marie Kennedy, eldest sister to President Kennedy and his Senator brothers. Indeed, we forgot about Tim Shriver's status as part of an American political dynasty. Instead, he was a nephew, a young man hoping to do some good in the world, and a person challenged and inspired by those he works with. Everyone in that room was able to connect with the human experiences of family, idealism, and kindness. We were touched by the simple strength of his Roman Catholic faith.

Tim Shriver shares a major storytelling train with Nido Qubein. He focuses on his personal story, not as a way of holding himself *above* the audience, but as a way of engaging *with* the audience.

Here is our favorite story of Shriver's, which he recounts in his 2014 book, *Fully Alive: Discovering What Matters Most.*

The story is about a professional photographer attending the opening of the 1995 Special Olympics. Amongst all the pageantry, the celebrations, the star-studded lineup, this professional spotted "a group of athletes clad in African dress," who had raised their disposable cameras to take pictures of President Clinton, who was positioned high atop the stadium. The Special Olympians were far away on the field. But something stood out to the photographer: the athletes all had their cameras facing backward. The photographer ran across the stadium to inform the athletes of their error. What happens next is a story that Shriver tells with great grace.

"Not knowing whether they spoke English, [the photographer] gestured to one of the athletes to lower his camera. 'You're trying to get a picture of the president?' he asked. The athlete didn't reply—just looked at him, apparently unable to speak or to understand. 'Yes, you're trying to get a picture of Clinton and he's way up there, but you have to turn the camera around. Let me show you.' The photographer flipped the direction of the camera. 'You see, you have to point the lens toward the president and then look through the viewfinder, and then you can get a good picture of him.

Oh, said the athlete, in clear and conversational English. Thank you, sir. But may I show you something? If you turn the camera around and hold your eye up to the viewfinder and look backward, it still works. It works like a telescope and you can see the president very clearly. So we're using these little cameras so we can get a good view of the president. But thank you for helping us."

Shriver tells this story to illustrate our assumptions about who is "disabled" and who is not. The African athletes in this anecdote, and the disabled in general, are not helpless. In fact, they are more capable than able-bodied people often give them credit for. Later in this book, we will further explore the power of using stories, as Shriver did here, to engage and captivate an audience.

Robert's Most Memorable Presentation: Bucky Fuller

Buckminster Fuller, it is fair to say, was one of the smartest human beings alive. He was an architect, inventor and systems theorist, and was the second president of the high-IQ group Mensa. He created and popularized concepts such as the geodesic dome, as well as the Dymaxion, a car that can drive, float, and fly. He is even responsible for several of the central terms we use today to conceive of our own existence—such as the idea of "Spaceship Earth."

I once attended a lecture and a conversation by Buckminster Fuller. The year was 1979, and "Bucky" Fuller was on a national tour with Werner Erhard, the businessman and academic. Erhard wanted to demonstrate how people could create possibilities out of nothing, just by speaking and thinking. There was no one better placed to demonstrate that reality than Bucky Fuller.

Bucky told us that if you focused on all the things he had created, all the amazing technology that he was the first to consider, then you missed the point of his life. Before his life as a science superstar, Bucky Fuller was a failed businessman, a grieving father who had lost his first child to polio and spinal meningitis, and penniless with no idea how to provide for his family. At age 32, he was drinking heavily and planning suicide.

As he was about to walk out into the icy waters of Lake Michigan, Fuller says a voice spoke directly to him, saying:

"You do not have the right to eliminate yourself. You do not belong to you. You belong to the Universe. Your significance will remain forever obscure to you, but you may assume that you are fulfilling your role if you apply yourself to converting your experiences to the highest advantage of others."[36]

This realization led to a shift in being that changed what Fuller was doing, and resulted in him becoming a world-renowned creator and inventor, a one-man intellectual treasure.

His story sticks with me to this day, because when he told us the stories of his failure, I could feel it. I don't think there was anybody in the room that day who hadn't had feelings like that, in some way.

Connecting with the Audience

All three of these presentations share certain commonalities: for example, these presenters focused on storytelling techniques and personal experiences rather than dry facts and figures. We will be studying, in-depth, what makes a good story later in this book.

Another point that we want to emphasize is this: all three presenters were world-renowned, recognized as leaders in their field. Yet the strength of their presentations derived not from the heights of their success but from their human experiences that connected them to the audience. Stories of bouncing back after failure, of overcoming adversity, of love and heartbreak and family . . . these are stories that every audience member intuitively understands and connects with. Recitation of a résumé may be impressive, but it does nothing to communicate your message.

It is counterintuitive that famous presenters derive some of their charisma precisely from the fact that they don't *need* to prove anything to anyone. They do not need to start a presentation with a recitation of their accomplishments, because people already know them. For the rest of us, it is far more tempting to begin a presentation or a discussion with a recap of our experiences and accomplishments. We may be insecure about our presentation, and we want our audience to understand why we are qualified to speak. That's all well and good, but remember that self-aggrandizement does not bring you closer to an audience. Instead, reminding the audience of your shared experiences is what connects you.

What is Authenticity?

Authenticity enhances your presence in two ways. For one, you feel comfortable that you can be who you are. You are not pretending. There is little to no fake façade that you must struggle to maintain. Therefore, little extraneous effort goes in this direction. Second, like an invisible wire taking up slack, authenticity draws the audience closer to you. The greater your authenticity, the shorter the distance between the microphone and the minds and hearts of your listeners.

Douglas Holladay, a former ambassador and a former Wall Street Investment banker, describes how genuine authenticity helps to close the distance gap. In his dealings with people of power and great wealth, Holladay noted an all-too common trait among these individuals, something he calls the law of unintended consequences. "The unintended consequences of great accomplishment are often isolation and unhappiness, especially when you don't know whom you can trust," he observes.

Along with colleagues Steve Case, former CEO of AOL and author of *The Third Wave: An Entrepreneur's Vision of the Future* (Simon & Schuster), and John Dalton, ex-Secretary of the Navy, Holladay formed PathNorth, an organization dedicated to helping leaders counter the "lonely at the top" syndrome. Through intimate get-togethers, shared experiences, and ego-less (as much as possible) dialogue, PathNorth focuses on providing a safe space for leaders to share their innermost thoughts and feelings.

Holladay defines authenticity as "the best version of yourself being as honest and real as you can be." He acknowledges that "authenticity demands that you become more real about your strengths and especially your weaknesses, setbacks, and failures. You become more honest when everything fits in: the good, bad and ugly."

Holladay teaches a very popular MBA class to students at Georgetown University. He notes that the students often enter with isolating-type behaviors, something he seeks to transform. He tells a revealing story:

> "When many of the engineers and up-and-coming executives enter my course, they are like dogs sniffing each other out, looking for places of weakness. After a few weeks, one of the more popular students stood up and remarked, 'I want to say something. I had a very severe stutter throughout junior high, high school and college. It was isolating. I had no friends. I was living in the shadows. I made up my mind to overcome this problem. I became student body president and had to speak all the time.'"

At the conclusion of these remarks, Holladay asked the class how they felt about this disclosure. The resounding answer from the classmates, was that they felt "safer." Because, according to Holladay, "When someone dares to share out of a place of weakness, we all feel safer."

Holladay notes that another major impediment to authenticity is the imposter syndrome, a term coined in 1978 by clinical psychologists Pauline Clance, PhD, and Suzanne Imes, PhD. [37] The researchers found that some high-achieving individuals, rather than being able to internalize and appreciate their accomplishments, experience a persistent fear of being exposed as a fraud. But it's not just the highly accomplished who suffer from this syndrome.

By focusing on our own insecurities—and comparing ourselves to others—we assume that others have it more together than we do. To make this point, Holladay talks of sharing a bottle of Bordeaux with Lawrence Rockefeller, whom he asked, "What's it like to be a Rockefeller?" Rockefeller's answer: "It is a recurrent dream in which I am at the bottom of a well and looking down at me is my father and my grandfather."

The ingredients of authenticity are like an old fashioned cook-off. Everyone has their own recipe, their combination of ingredients, blended in a unique fashion, and prepared with unique intentionality. We do know that there are some common ingredients in all the recipes. Being authentic means accepting yourself; being willing to learn more from your weaknesses than your strengths; letting go of judgment and the preconceived notion that you have all the answers.

Social Media Authenticity

Having personally addressed thousands of healthcare and business professionals, we are always amazed at the great difficulty most have with the "elevator speech." This is a 30-60 second summary in answer to the question, "What's so special about you that I (or my family members or friends) should make an appointment to see you?" Many professionals are not clear on the type(s) of customers they want to attract. This lack of clarity and focus is often on display on their websites and in their social media, most visibly in their LinkedIn profiles. With more than 380 million members, LinkedIn is the most popular social network for professionals. When many of us Google our names, our LinkedIn profile appears at the top of the list, often ahead of our own websites. Even potential clients who are referred by friends will glance at your LinkedIn page (in addition to usually checking out reviews and your website) before scheduling an appointment.

The first step to creating social media authenticity is to get clear on whom you want to attract. If for example, you are seeking to influence your professional colleagues, then a more academic tone ("let me tell you why I should speak at your next conference") is appropriate. In this situation, your online presence can tout your credentials, achievements, and other accolades that will influence conference organizers, book publishers, society members, etc.

The vast majority of professionals, however, are seeking to attract customers. And while some draw from a national and international audience, you will find that most of your customers likely live within a 30-mile radius of your place of business.

So what does authentic social media communication look like to them?

Let's begin by telling you what we believe it is not: a third person recitation of credentials, skewed to features, and disregarding benefits. Below is a composite of this type of profile, represented by a fictional physician who is trying to build his cash-pay surgical and non-surgical aesthetic business by attracting new clients.

Dr. John Smith is a board-certified otorhinolaryngologist and Head and Neck Surgeon. He went to medical school at The University of XYZ, did his ENT residency at XYZ, and then completed his fellowship training with noted aesthetic surgeon Dr. John Doe, in Beverly Hills. Dr. Smith specializes in aesthetic facial surgery. His office features the latest lasers from the major companies. He is a one of the top injectors in the country. His office is now accepting new patients.

Contrast the above with this one:

Have you ever wondered which are the best treatments for *you* to turn back the clock on facial aging and look your absolute best? I take great pride in answering this question, and go over the options and choices during your first non-hurried consultation. I'll show you realistic images of the results you can expect. Your answer may lie in skin rejuvenation to eliminate fine lines, get rid of brown and red spots and tighten the skin; subtle additions of filler or muscle-relaxing injections to eliminate frown lines; or surgical procedures to reshape your nose, jowls or neck. Here's what my patients have to say about the care we provide: www.changewell.com/testimonials

Which one rings of greater authenticity? Creates a sense of practitioner presence? Addresses concerns? Highlights benefits? Provides social proof? Which is more likely to result in the prospective patient calling for an appointment?

To create a more authentic online presence, begin by answering these questions:

- To whom are you addressing your profile?
- What is it you want them to do as a result of reading about you?
- What tone do you want to set? How warm, crisp, authoritative?

- What benefits do you provide for the reader? And are these the ones they are looking for?
- What voice will you be using? A third-person voice for credentialing to peers or a first-person voice to attract customers?
- What is unique about your focus, and practice approach?
- What is your practice philosophy?
- Is there anything special about your office layout, staff or culture? Finally,
- Who should write your profile?

We have found that most professionals, and the staff to whom they delegate this task, lack the ability to adequately capture the professional's presence and why others should be drawn to her. We recommend you seek out a local public relations firm, marketing or social media agency. We often direct our customers to use the profile writing services of everyonelinked.com, a San Diego group that draws clients from around the US. You can find other groups by searching for "Consultant for LinkedIn Profile." Where? LinkedIn, of course. Having a consultant rewrite your LinkedIn profile for a modest fee is a great first test of their abilities to assist you.

Being Persuasive

The word "persuade" come from the Latin "per" which means "thoroughly" and "suadere" which means "to advise or urge." To persuade means to thoroughly advise or urge. It appears as if persuasion is the art of getting others to do what we want them to do. But what if it's not that at all? What if it's actually the art of helping others do what they want to do—to do what serves them best?

Healthcare practitioners are often caught between a rock and a hard place. They know the important role that diet and exercise play in avoiding illness, yet they also know that preaching and scolding will not help patients make lifestyle changes. In the course of a week, clinicians have told patients about the value of diet and exercise dozens of times. Tired of saying and hearing these same words, the practitioner truncates the message, now delivered as a bland "should" or "ought to," or worse yet, avoids bringing up the topic all together.

Physicians also know that prescribing antibiotics for viral colds and bronchitis is ineffective, and in fact, contributes to the growing tide of antibiotic resistance. However, examine the antibiotic prescribing habits of primary care physicians for cold and flu, and you'll find that they give out more prescriptions in the afternoon then they do in the morning.[38] They are clearly tired of "selling" the non-efficacy idea to their inappropriately demanding patients.

Or take the growing opioid epidemic. The problem stems in part from lax physician prescribing patterns, but these same physicians know that saying "no" to a chronic pain patient may get them a bad review on social media, or lower their status on the popular physician rating sites. In addition, many physicians have been trained to identify pain as the "fifth vital sign," and to do all that is necessary to make patients comfortable.

When physicians operate in these ways, they are not serving the patient; they are (wearily) serving themselves. They put concerns about how they will be perceived ahead of what is truly in the best interest of their patients. When this happens, physicians stop "selling" the idea that exercise and diet is the best medicine, that antibiotics don't affect the common cold, and that non-narcotic options for chronic pain need to be explored.

We tell our healthcare and non-healthcare clients that this kind of thinking is based on a very common and complete misunderstanding of what "selling" really is. But it is also based on another essential truth: the more we push, the more resistance we create. So, how do we persuade powerfully and effectively? How do we get our point across without creating a defensive, resistant client?

In the healthcare world, a technique known as **motivational interviewing** has sprung up, designed to help patients overcome their ambivalence to change and to help practitioners enable the change process. While arising from the healthcare field, it can work in any profession or service business. Developed by psychologists William Miller, PhD, and Stephen Rollnick, PhD, motivational interviewing combines the skills of good listening with empathy and focused questions to spark a process of patient/client-centered inquiry. [39] Rather than immediately prescribe, the clinician is encouraged to ask open-ended questions to tease out what a patient is willing to commit to, and what they are willing to do. Here are some general examples of such questions:

- "What would you like to see different about your current situation?"
- "What difficulties have you encountered trying to make this change?"
- "Of all the possibilities we've discussed, where would you like to begin?"

Clearly, in the healthcare setting, selling behavior change has its own special dynamics. How might this process of greater engagement and enhanced motivation work beyond the clinician, for any and all of us who want to be more persuasive?

How to Sell Well

You have probably heard a great sales presentation involving a quality product or service. Rather than feeling forced, coerced, manipulated or used, you might have bought, signed up, or enrolled with a sense of excitement, even gratitude, at the benefit or opportunity you have seized. Typically in these transactions, rather than feeling victimized by a slick operator, we feel that the seller is a friend.

Indeed, the truly great sellers, whose promises meet our expectations, are those who help us recognize and activate ideas we already have. In many cases, it's their sales presentation that gets us to realize that these ideas are already alive within us— looking for a way to be expressed and realized.

Such presenters don't "handle objections;" they remove barriers. Rather than "selling us," they "help us buy." The process is not adversarial in any way. It's almost as if the seller starts out "on your side" and guides you through the process of closing the deal. It's not an argument. It's a respectful service. And for that reason we say:

Persuasion is a by-product of presence.

It all starts with listening. In her bestseller *Presence: Bringing Your Boldest Self to Your Biggest Challenges,* social psychologist Amy Cuddy, PhD, Associate Professor at Harvard Business School, suggests we intentionally give up the illusion of power that comes from us speaking, preaching, and teaching, and just listen.

When we do that, a host of benefits arise. Others begin to trust us. We get useful information. We begin to see where we have shared goals and that makes us allies instead of adversaries. Because we know what our customers need, we develop solutions they want to buy. And because we've done all of that listening, our customers are now magically interested in listening to us.

Features and Benefits

A classic sales presentation has features and benefits. A feature is a physical fact about the product or service. The benefit is what it does for the customer. One of the most persistent stumbling blocks in the selling process is the failure to clearly connect product features to customer benefits.

All too often we think it is enough to say: "Graduated from Harvard Business School," or "Has a 380 horsepower V8 engine," or "Twice the processing power of most laptops." These are features. While they might be true, it's not clear why they are valuable or relevant to the customer.

Some customers can translate the presence of a feature into something of benefit to them. Most can't. A sales presentation that is heavy on features often leaves customers confused. They even think it "insults my intelligence." By that they mean: "I'm smart, but I didn't understand what he was talking about. He has not made himself clear."

If your sales presentation is about a product or service, here is a process you can use to make your presentation more persuasive:

1. List all of your product features.
2. Based on customer input, prioritize the list of features, putting the ones that are most important to customers on the top of your list. When presenting features and benefits, start with the features at the top of the list.
3. Put a big star next to features that give you a unique competitive advantage. Be sure to emphasize these to

explain how they make your product different and therefore better.

4. Create a clear benefit statement by using connecting phrases like
    a. "so that you can…"
    b. "in order to…"
    c. "which lets you…"
    d. "that's important because…"

Your feature/benefit statements will look like this:

"Jack is a recent graduate from Harvard Business School. He'll be handling your account exclusively and **that's important because** he brings you the type of sophisticated management expertise you want and deserve."

"The Z380 has a 380 hp V8 engine **so that you can** cruise in comfort and yet have plenty of reserve power to handle any driving situation."

"It has twice the processing power of most laptops, **which lets you** edit video four times faster than on the device you currently use."

In some cases, you might want to reverse the order and lead with a benefit.

"Raise your hands. How many of you dentists have had patients express concern about possible damage from dental X-rays? Most of you. And I'm sure your staff has the same concerns, right? Well, we have a way to eliminate that risk for you, your staff, and your patients. Let me introduce you to our new digital X-Ray system." This presentation leads with the benefit and then reveals how it is accomplished.

Stated or unstated, every single presentation involves selling of some kind. You may not be asking for money in return for a product or service, but you do want to get your point across, champion an idea or position, convey important information, or inspire others to take action. If you are in healthcare, financial services, a non-profit activity, or any other serving profession, your presentation is imbued with deep meaning.

Your message may be just the trigger that dispels misconceptions, ignites behavior change, informs about resources, or enables action for an acute or chronic condition. Think of your ideas as product features. Create clear benefit statements that connect your ideas to customer needs. Show how your ideas result in benefits. Use the presentation techniques we discuss in the next chapter.

Few things can be more rewarding than delivering a meaningful presentation in which you share something that you believe is very important to others. Always approach your presentation with the gravitas it deserves. You are embarking on a noble adventure. You may never again have the opportunity to be with the people in the audience; this may be your only chance to reach out to them.

Now that you are armed with intention and passion, it's time to turn our attention to the skills that you will need to captivate and motivate your audience. However, as you reflect on what it takes to get you on the MAP, we encourage you to keep the following in mind:

You can learn techniques for becoming memorable and persuasive....

But only life can teach you how to be authentic.

Chapter 4

Master the Presentation Basics

"The speaker catches fire
looking at their faces.
His words
jump down to stand
In listener's places."
— Langston Hughes

Anyone who has worked with a fitness trainer is familiar with their nearly universal approach: a combination of cardio, strength exercises, and stretching. The trainer guides you through your program, varying duration and intensity of each element to meet your objectives. You probably won't get into good shape unless you engage in these basic activities.

The same principle applies to one aspect of presence: presentation skills. If you want to get your presentations in better shape, you'll want to master some basics. The presentation is the arena in which you demonstrate your charisma, set forth your intention, grab and hold the audience's attention, and ideally move attendees toward your point of view. Here is our stepwise training regimen.

#1. Understand your Audience

Every patient/client/customer presentation should be centered around meeting and exceeding their expectations. This is the definition of quality, an aspect of service delivery that is defined by the customer experience. You deliver value when the experience exceeds the "cost," measured as money and/or time. In order to meet and exceed the expectations of your audience, and deliver value, you will want to gather as much background information as possible to organize and fine-tune your presentation. If you are planning to conduct a talk or workshop in your facility with your clientele, you already have sufficient background to prepare well. However, if you are asked by a third party or conference organizer to present, or if you are doing a sales presentation, you want to make certain to get the answers to some or all of these questions:

- Why was I asked to speak?
- Who will be attending and what do I need to know about them?
- What would you like the audience to come away with from my session?
- What other speakers has this group been exposed to and how were they received?
- How technically/scientifically/medically literate is this group?
- How much time will I have to present my talk?
- How will participants be seated? Theater style, rounds, lecture tables?
- What time of day will the session occur?

- What color is the backdrop behind me?
- What AV equipment is available? Will I have access to a lavaliere or an untethered hand held mike?
- Will we be using my laptop or a conference laptop? Do I have the necessary connectors and the presentation in the correct software version?
- Is audio available through an HDMI connection if I choose to show a video, or do I need to bring small speakers?

Getting answers to these basic questions can set the context for a focused presentation and help you avoid making an easily preventable mistake. Furthermore, mistakes in logistics can overshadow your great content. There are some other preparatory steps you can take, depending upon the specifics of the situation:

- **Unfamiliar territory.** If you are speaking to a group you know little about, for example, an association, educational institution or corporation, try to arrange some time in advance to meet or speak by phone with one or more representative participants. Have them brief you on the culture and dynamics of the organization. This way, you'll be able to learn acronyms and obtain shared audience experiences that you can incorporate into your talk.
- **Timing.** Whenever possible, get to a presentation early—preferably at break time before your talk—and meet some of the participants. Learn their names. Ask them what they'd like to get out of your talk. When you deliver your presentation you will no longer be looking out at a sea of unfamiliar faces. You can initially direct your remarks to those attendees

whom you have briefly gotten to know. This helps put you at ease. Depending upon the nature and formality of your presentation, it is always helpful to be able to relate personally to one or more participants and acknowledge them in the course of your talk.

- **Cultural Sensitivity.** If appropriate, attune your presentation to meet the needs of different cultures. When Mark gives a presentation to a group that primarily speaks another language, he will often memorize a paragraph in that language, telling the audience how honored he is to be there, and apologize for his poor speaking skills in their native tongue. Do not assume that people who might be able to read English understand the spoken word as well. The main takeaway for cross-cultural comprehension is to speak S-L-O-W-L-Y in your native tongue, even painfully so. Use smaller, easier-to-understand terms. If you are going to have near simultaneous translation, plan to reduce your content by 20-40% so the non-English speaking attendees can follow along and you will not run over on time.

- **The Hostile Audience.** If you know in advance that your message will be delivered to a potentially hostile audience, prepare by making a list of the questions you believe you might encounter. More importantly, be prepared to be the target of negative emotions, regardless of whether you are merely the messenger, or are actually the instigator of change. Facing hostile audiences is never easy. In the face of an onslaught, you must do a handful of things: listen without attempting to prove others wrong, show that you understand their point of view, have patience, and control your autonomic nervous system so you don't lose your temper. In Chapter 8, you'll find some coherence techniques to help you stay calm and collected.

#2. Organize for Simplicity

One axiom remains true for all presentations: less is more. While each situation is different, in general you will be best served by reducing the number of slides, the text on the slides, and the number of syllables of the words. We've all had the experience of suffering through "death by PowerPoint." If you want to communicate with greater clarity, integrity, appeal, and wisdom, you must naturally be more restrained, and yes, more simple. Resist the temptation to put two hours of slides—no matter how great they are—into a 30-minute talk.

For those of us who present at conferences, it has increasingly become the norm for conference organizers to include a set of your slides in the handout material. This has led to presenters creating text heavy slides that reference the scientific or technical literature, ostensibly for attendees to refer back to the articles. Presenters feel that they must cram their slides full of the key points from the literature.

This type of presentation does not extend well to a more general audience. In reality, it doesn't even extend well to peers. For starters, people have difficulty processing information if it comes at them simultaneously in verbal and written forms. As we mentioned in Chapter 2 (The Neuroscience of Presence), we process spoken and written words along the same cognitive channel. So, when you overload people with text on a slide, they can either listen to you, or read the slides, but they can't do both. And if the purpose of the presentation is solely to convey the content on the slides, why do participants even need you to deliver the talk? They could just read the slides.

The spoken part of your presentation has to do more than just reiterate the bullet points from your slides. For instance, your speech can contextualize your message; inspire others to adopt your point of view; formulate disparate ideas into a new paradigm; or share your professional experience. You can always put your research-based, statistics-laden, referenced material into a separate handout.

When and wherever possible, emphasize images, and visualizations of quantitative information in their simplest formats. For hints and tips, view the SlideShare by Garr Reynolds, author of *Presentation Zen.*

http://www.slideshare.net/garr/sample-slides-by-garr-reynolds/5-beforeafter and heed his words:

> "First, make slides that reinforce your words, not repeat them. Create slides that demonstrate, with emotional proof, that what you're saying is true, not just accurate. No more than six words on a slide. EVER."

With more digital tools at our command than ever before, we have entered what some call the "Presentation Generation." Impactful visuals can help you get your message across more easily, but they can only augment, not supplant, your ability to speak passionately, clearly, and concisely about a given topic. Nor can great visuals alone captivate and motivate your audience.

#3. Rehearse Well

Have you ever watched a really skilled comedian and left the performance thinking that he or she is a natural? We often assume that comedy comes easily and spontaneously to such performers. But this assumption is wrong. Every single line that a skillful comedian utters has been rehearsed, dissected, tested, and modified for maximum impact. The entire presentation, though it may seem totally off-the-cuff and spontaneous, is anything but.

It takes time to "own" a given presentation. It takes time to get the pacing, the storytelling, the humor, and the emotion dialed in. The major advantage of slides is their ability to help you organize and pace your presentation. Try to organize your message around no more than five, but preferably three, key points. These are anchors for your presentation, and you can build your preparation around them.

Many people find it helpful to practice in front of a full-length mirror. This can also serve to help coordinate movements and hand gestures. Others find great value in doing a first-time talk in front of an audience of friends and staff. Another approach is to do a dry run by using a Chartpak and some colored markers. As you move through the talk, draw the pictures and graphs needed to complement your words. This way, when you come to the charts in your PowerPoint or Keynote presentation, you will be assured that you can understand and explain them.

Video can be incredibly helpful in your preparation. Taping, and then viewing (ideally the next day), a few of your early attempts will help you identify unclear explanations, as well as problems with transitions, timing, or pacing that are easily fixable with practice.

The real payoff lies in mastering a presentation. You "perform" to a new audience each time you give it, but the presentation itself can stay—in whole or in part—the same.

#4. Use Preparation Time Wisely

All presentations require preparation. If you were to create a pie chart to demonstrate how and where you should spend your time in the weeks, days and hours before your presentation, what would it look like? How best should you allocate your time?

Our answer is simple. Focus on identifying some really great bread and *trust that the sandwich will build itself.* The bread in this analogy is the open and close of your talk; the ingredients are the supporting points. As we discussed in Chapter 2, research shows that your presentation's beginning and ending will likely be the segments that your audience will remember the most. These are the parts that our "sandwich" approach emphasizes. Here's how this preparation might look:

1. **Top piece of bread.** During the week before your talk, when you are working out, showering, or just waking up in the morning, craft, rehearse and really nail the first two to three minutes of your presentation. These are the times when people are at their most creative. Get to the point where you can deliver your opening from memory without any notes. Visualize the intended reactions of your audience. Identify where and for how long you intend to strategically pause for emphasis.

2. **Bottom piece of bread.** Spend time memorizing the one-minute ending. Concentrate on "sticking the landing," a skill we describe in detail in Chapter 7: Hone Your Story. Finish on a high note by displaying confidence in tone and body posture. If you are making a commercial pitch, get very clear on "the ask." What is it you want your participants to *do* as a result of your

presentation?

3. **The ingredients.** Trust that, for the middle portion of the presentation, "the sandwich will make itself." Organize your content into three to five key points. Include the supporting data in an easy-to-understand fashion, or a supremely motivational one, depending upon your audience. We have found that many speakers are most comfortable discussing the middle portion of a presentation. This often includes information about themselves, the company, their research, or technology.

There are many advantages to this type of organization and preparation, not the least of which is the feeling of confidence you achieve by getting started well and finishing strong.

#5. Win Before You Get on Stage

Imagine this: you've been invited to speak before a large group of your peers at a national meeting. Most of the attendees are unfamiliar with you, your work, and your background. The meeting coordinator says that she will be introducing you and asks that you send her a short paragraph or two that she will read. What will you send her? Does it even matter?

If you're like 90% of presenters, you are going to list your credentials. Where you went to school, where you trained, some details about your specialty, maybe a few acknowledgements or awards you've garnered. Perhaps the titles of one or more books or articles you've written.

Sure, you could do this. But you know what? You've just missed an enormous opportunity to win your audience over before you even open your mouth.

Let's take a closer look at two fictional written introductions, in this case relating to a presentation on women's health and integrative medicine. Here's the typical one:

> Dr. Smith is a board-certified Obstetrician and Gynecologist in Miami, Florida. She trained at XYZ Medical School and did her residency at XYZ Medical Center. She has been in practice for eight years and is a proud recipient of Miami's 100 Great Doctors Award. She has authored chapters in several textbooks and been involved in studies on inflammation and the microbiome.

Now let's examine the second intro:

> Our next speaker is a champion for women's healthcare. She has pioneered a unique approach to addressing functional diseases by bringing a deep understanding of inflammation, the microbiome and hormones to her work. She will be guiding you through the theory, the practice, and the pros and cons of her approach. More, importantly, you will leave with a practical, step-wise method to better serve your female patients. LADIES AND GENTLEMAN, PLEASE JOIN ME IN WELCOMING DR. MARY SMITH.

What's the difference between these two approaches?

- Which is more captivating?
- Which generates excitement and anticipation of what's to come?
- Which holds more promise for the participant and less praise for the presenter?
- But WAIT? Don't I have to provide my credentials to show I'm an authority?

Sure—that's what you've got print for. You always have the option and opportunity to work your credentials into the body of your presentation, sprinkling the narrative with morsels of flavor. For example, "When I conducted my fellowship with Dr. X at the Mass General, he always reinforced...."

So the next time you are asked to provide your introduction, spice it up a bit, make the narrative more focused on benefits than features, and "win" over your audience before you even make it to the podium.

#6. Hook 'Em Quick

As we explored in Chapter 2, attention spans are short and getting shorter. When you present to an audience, you've got to capture their attention and halt the meanderings of their wandering minds. As we noted earlier, if you win or lose audience attention in the first eight seconds of your presentation, what should you say in those eight seconds? The best way to engage your audience is to paint a picture.

While we spend much of our time speaking in words and figures, people receive messages as emotions and images.

One of the best engagement tools is to **open your presentation or discussion with a simple, but powerful word: Imagine**. Then go on to paint a picture from days past, present or future. Go for bold imagery. For example:

"**Imagine...** It's your daughter's first day of college. You've driven her to her new school. It's just the two of you sitting in the car. She's about to leap into uncharted waters. As you glance her way you can barely hold back the tears. It was just yesterday when she had her first swim lesson. Today she's got a full ride scholarship courtesy of her backstroke. All the early mornings, the two-a-days, the ever present smell of chlorine in her hair, and on her skin; the bake sales and car washes to raise money for the swim team. So much hard work and sacrifice. When you look over at her, you see the tears, and you know it was all so worth it."

We teach three other techniques to effectively open your presentation.

The first is what we call **Eyedropper.** A series of words ... or short phrases ... delivered with significant pauses. Like drops of liquid, they fall on the ears of the audience. And it works especially well if the connection is not yet clear. For example:

A laboratory experiment...

A random gust of wind...

A game changing medical discovery...

This is the story of the discovery of penicillin.

A second technique is to **Mine the Audience**. We do this in the beginning of our *Enhance Your Presence* training program when we ask: "What was the best presentation you ever saw, who gave it, and why was it so great?" The key is to ask the audience a question they can answer, and no matter what answer they give —it serves the purpose of your talk. The pitfall is to ask a question that only you can answer. That results in embarrassed silence.

Finally, here's a technique we call **Once Upon a Time...** Tell a story that relates powerfully to your topic. Use the present tense if possible. Bring the character to life right next to you on stage by telling the story in vivid, descriptive language that allows your audience to visualize what's happening. Here's a story Robert relates that sets the stage for a presentation on the importance of giving a patient the correct diagnosis.

> It's a funeral home in Bangor, Maine. It's my father's wake. A woman named Sheila is sympathetically holding my hand. "You're Dr. Hughes' son." Yes, I am, how did you know my dad? "Well, he saved my life....When I met him I had been told I had three months to live. That was 18 years ago." Sheila's problem was serious, but not life-threatening, and my dad performed the operation that fixed it and restored her quality of life. Best of all, he saved her from having to endure the wrong treatment.

#7. Attend to Your Non-Verbals

The art of the theater developed in classical Athens in the sixth century B.C. What has remained constant over the last 2,500 years is the power of the live performance. Human beings are wired for face-to-face contact. Real magic can take place when a speaker's words, tone, and pacing unite with nonverbal physical gestures: eye contact, facial expressions, gestures and body posture. One of our colleagues describes this amalgam as "resonance."

According to Webster's New World Dictionary, "Resonance is the effect produced when the natural vibration frequency of a body is greatly amplified by reinforcing vibrations at the same frequency from another body." Perhaps the simplest example of resonance can be found by the close proximity of two similarly pitched tuning forks. Striking the one will generate vibrations and sound in the other.

There's a lot more being transferred in a presentation than just content. In the first two minutes of your talk your audience is picking up dozens of subconscious clues that determine whether they will understand and be inspired by your remarks.

Find Your Position of Power

Bodies radiate energy. We can observe this phenomenon as we observe the collapsed posture of individuals who are depressed, the shaky movements of anxious individuals, or the quiet confidence and alignment of a yoga or mediation teacher.

You can find your position of power by standing up straight and aligning your spine. Bring your shoulders back and down. Uplift your sternum by imagining a wire lifting it to the ceiling. Straighten your head and tilt your chin slightly down. Arrange your pelvis in a neutral position.

Spend a bit of time in front of a full-length mirror to identify how and what you can do to find this starting point. Then, while maintaining this position, allow your body to relax. Soften your grip and remove tension from your forehead, eyes and jaw. You can always work with a posture or yoga coach to provide some necessary feedback.

Sync Your Gestures

If you observe a conversation between two people who know each other well, chances are their arms and hands don't just lie stiffly by their sides like dead fish. Most of us naturally use our hands and arms to make our words more persuasive and intimate.

Research suggests that gestures also make our words more memorable, whether we're talking to one person or to three hundred. A recent analysis by researchers at Kalamazoo College looked at 63 existing studies focusing on gestures. In aggregate, these studies showed that accompanying verbal information with hand gestures was a significant aid to listeners' comprehension, learning, and memory.[40]

Similarly, recent research has showed that students retain more information, retain it for longer, and can apply it to more scenarios when they are taught by teachers using hand gestures.[41] So, whether you are giving a training presentation to a large group or teaching an individual patient about her condition, your audience will better retain the information you convey when you use gestures.

That's not the only benefit to talking with your hands. Making gestures as you speak actually helps *you* find the right words, too. A study at Queen Margaret University College tested this by restricting arm and hand use in some participants, while allowing others to use their arms and hands normally, during a conversation. The researchers found that subjects who weren't allowed to use their arms were less verbally articulate in conversation than those who could use their arms: the former group paused, stumbled, and repeated themselves more.[42]

This isn't necessarily to say that you should randomly or constantly gesture when you give a talk. Rather, your hand gestures should be purposeful and precise. They should be employed to reinforce a point. For example, if you want to illustrate something increasing—such as the size of your business—you could move hands outward from a centered position near your chest (Fig. 3).

Fig. 3

To emphasize an emotional point or something you deeply believe, touching you heart with one or two hands amplifies the message (Fig. 4)

Fig. 4

You can also use your fingers as counting points, especially when you tell the audience, that you'd like to leave them with, "Three key take-homes." You can count these off on your fingers (Fig. 5)

Fig. 5

Gestures can also reflect time or movement (Fig 6). For example, you can direct people in time by gesturing about the past...and the future.

Fig. 6

When you use gestures, you must also make certain that they are culturally appropriate. For example, in the United States, the okay sign means "all right;" in some other countries, this innocuous gesture takes on an insulting meaning.

Keep in mind that when you are on video, if you are in a tight or medium shot, you'll want to keep your gestures to a minimum. Your hands should stay within a box that is between your belt and shoulders and half way to the maximum reach of your outstretched arms. Avoid reaching out with your hands directly to the camera; this has the effect of distorting perspective, so your hands become disproportionately large and potentially distracting.

Make Eye Contact

Establishing eye contact is essential for resonating with your audience. Research indicates that we tend to find people who make eye contact with us to be more likable and attractive.[43] We also remember more information from speakers who lock gazes with us on a regular basis. This holds true whether we're watching a presenter in person or over video.[44] Scholars have suggested that this greater recall effect may occur because eye contact acts as an arousal stimulus, signaling to our brains, "pay attention!" and "remember this!"[45]

During the course of your presentation, you can employ three techniques.

Scan the Audience. This is essential in a large presentation when people are spread out horizontally and vertically as well. Divide the audience into quadrants and periodically direct your gaze in the direction of each quadrant.

Look for the light ups. As you drive home one of your key points, scan the room to see who seems to resonate with your remarks. Such a person is smiling, nodding, or giving you some other sign of affirmation. Linger just a moment on their face and strengthen the connection you are feeling.

Draw people out. Many presenters feel that they have to always be the energy source and put energy into the crowd. But there are more of them out there and you are just one person. So, in fact, you can tap into the energy of the crowd. This can be accomplished by a combination of eye contact and the "draw out gesture," which is an underhanded point out directed at one or more attendees (Fig. 7).

Fig. 7

This is simple to master. Rather than point your hand and fingers as if they were a gun, rotate your hand so that your palm faces upwards and fingers are relaxed, as if holding a fragile bird. With this opened hand, you can use a beckoning motion to engage people.

Use Movement Wisely

The size of the stage and audience can influence how much you move. For example, when Mick Jagger performs at a major stadium, it is not uncommon to see him run totally across the stage or out into the audience. When he performs the same song in a club, or a more intimate setting, his motion is naturally restricted.

The late-night television hosts have perfected the walk as well. Because their image is confined to the tighter dimensions of a video screen, they are much more conservative. They step forward and back, but they don't rock or sway. The latter behaviors become a "visual hiccup" that distract from your talk.

It can be helpful to set three or four spots on a stage and practice moving to each area. This is particularly important if you want to address your remarks to the entire audience.

Your delivery will be more impactful if you also sync some of your movements to your narrative. For example, if you are telling a story that goes back and forth in time, move several steps backwards to illustrate the past, and several steps forward to illustrate the future.

One more thing: always get a handheld microphone or lavaliere and try to never get trapped behind the podium.

#8 Fine-tune Your Instrument

Think of your presentation as a symphony. You are the composer, conductor, and principal soloist. Your instrument is your voice. As the composer and conductor, your job is to create music that your soloist can skillfully perform within the capabilities of his or her instrument.

Let's put aside the metaphor for some plain talk. No one can bear a speech delivered in either a monotone or a high-pitched screech. Ideally, your voice should be rich, warm, and smooth. Your vocal energy should be relaxed and confident but not sleepy, energetic but not tense or frantic.

Here are some techniques to generate a more pleasing presentation:

Speak in your natural register. Your most powerful and pleasing speaking voice will most likely be pitched in the lower to middle part of your natural register. This is typically the home of your warmest, richest, and most relaxed tones. This voice will sound confident and relaxed, with plenty of room for you to turn up the energy to make a point or express exuberance.

This works for most people, but not all. Some voices don't have a lot of texture or character in their middle range. They sound better at a slightly higher pitch because it makes the words easier to understand. Find your vocal sweet spot and practice it so you know where it resides.

Come from your chest. Your most pleasing and powerful voice will usually come from your chest, not your head or your throat, and it will be powered by abdominal breathing. However, when you have a bad case of nerves before a talk, abdominal breathing will not seem like a good idea. Use the "Sarnoff Squeeze" which we describe in Chapter 5, Slay the Fear Dragon.

Adjust volume accordingly. How loud should you be? If you are using a microphone, remember that "micro" means "small" and "phone" means "sound." Don't yell into a microphone. If there is a sound engineer, he will just turn your volume down. If you'll be speaking to a convention, find a voice that you would use to address a group in a small- to medium-sized room. Let the microphone make it big enough to be heard.

Vary your volume. This adds interest. But keep in mind that if you soften your vocal texture to a whisper, you must boost your volume. This is paradoxical. You will need to experiment with the idea of softening the sound of your voice to create a whisper, while simultaneously powering that sound with all the energy of a very loud yell. That's a "stage whisper," a soft sound that carries to the back of the theater.

Don't shout. A loud voice is not necessarily a friendly or persuasive voice. Some of the ugliest voices are those of politicians trying to address a large crowd. They raise their pitch, increase their volume, and tighten down their vocal chords to mistakenly add force and power. This makes them sound tense, combative, and angry rather than excited, like they are on the losing side of a bitter argument. The result is that the crowd feels like they are being yelled at—because they are. And after a while, these speakers end up with hoarse, permanently damaged vocal chords.

Practice talking with the intention of finding a comfortable, persuasive, relaxed but energized way of speaking. Video-record your practice sessions and get feedback. Once you've found your sound, practice it until it becomes second nature.

Script Your Talk

Your script (yes, your written script) should be written to be read aloud. Write for the ear more than the eye. What looks good on paper frequently sounds artificial when you speak it. For starters, this means keep sentences short because your speaker (you) must find convenient places to breathe.

Mark up your script with performance cues. We indicate breaks either by starting a new paragraph or with a double slash: // That means STOP. PAUSE. RESUME.

We like to indicate shorter pauses... like that... by using the three dots called ellipsis. When words should be read as a chunk, we like to highlight them in color. When delivering your talk, read in chunks of phrases... using expression and pauses... to tie ideas together... or.... split them apart. (We're over-using ellipsis here to make a point. Read this paragraph aloud, pausing when you see the three dots and you'll understand what we're intending.)

You can dramatically improve your presentation skills with voice coaching and training. It need not be a drawn-out affair. Speech therapists and acting coaches can help you get over your bad habits and provide you with personal feedback.

But here are a few things you can start working on right now, before your first appointment with a speaking coach:

1. Lose the "lame language." These are the all-too-common verbal distractions in your delivery. These are the words and phrases that are unconvincingly feeble. They dilute your message and detract from your credibility. These range from too many "Umms" and "Ahs" to the ubiquitous "You know" or even the overworked "I think..." construction. After all, if you didn't think, you wouldn't have anything to say. People get in the bad habit of resorting to these sounds and phrases because they provide time for the speaker to compose his or her next idea.

One remedy for lame language is the intentional pause. (More about this later in the chapter.) When you come to the completion of your idea, instead of saying "Umm" or "Ah" to buy time, simply pause. Allow what you have just said to get soaked up by the audience. Take a breath. Maybe smile or make eye contact...and then move purposefully on to your next idea. You will come across as more authentic if you also try to cut down on trite business—or professorial speak. "At the end of the day," "In my humble opinion," "After careful consideration of the facts." It takes a concerted effort to break free of your linguistic bad habits.

Here's a tip: Put a rubber band around your wrist, and for the next three days, every time you catch yourself using lame language, give yourself a tweak. Or try the tip Mark employed with his pre-teen daughter a decade ago when he carpooled with her Southern California friends. He told her that whenever anyone in the car uttered an inappropriate "like," twenty-five cents would be deducted from her allowance. The "likes" became few and far between.

2. You wrote it—now rehearse it. Notes on paper are a musical score, but they're not music. Music is notes in the air. Likewise, you wrote your speech to be heard, so rehearse it aloud—preferably in front of a video camera where you can see your facial expressions, body language, and gestures. Pay attention to how variations in tone and pacing can add meaning and variety, greatly increasing the listenability of your presentation. Ask a colleague for feedback and incorporate the feedback into your next rehearsal.

3. Practice varying the pitch of your voice. In the course of normal conversation, most of us use a very narrow range of pitch. Yet we all have the ability to use the lower, middle, or higher ranges. You don't want to get stuck in one register; you want to vary your pitch to hold the audience's attention. Many excellent short videos can be found on YouTube by searching "How to Improve Your Voice, or "How to Improve Your Pitch."

4. Make imaginative use of sound. One of our favorite words is "onomatopoeia." It refers to a word that phonetically imitates the sound it represents. One set of examples is animal noises like "meow" or "quack." But there are other words that can be brought to life by the way you say them. The word "sprinkle." Say it aloud with no expression. Now say it again and this time, illustrate it two ways: with a sprinkling motion of your hands and with a deliberate twinkle in your voice. This is what actors do. They bring words to life in the air by body, hand and voice.

Look for words with a sound, and phrase them in a way that adds a dramatic touch. A phrase like "A hush fell over the crowd..." could come to life if you combine the sound of the word with a pause, a change in volume, and a hand gesture: "A husshhhhhh... fell over the crowd." Notice the difference here: "I would wake up and drag myself into the office." Versus "I would wake up... and dragggggg myself into the office."

Write your script, review it, make performance notes, and practice. Ask for feedback. And practice some more.

Find ways to illustrate your ideas with your unique combination of voice, tone, pacing, inflection and performance. Use everything at your command to bring your ideas powerfully to life.

5. Vary your pacing. Mark says he learned many of his presentation skills from Walt Disney. Well, not from Walt in the flesh, but rather, from repeatedly watching the scene in Disney's *Fantasia* that is accompanied by Beethoven's *Pastoral* Symphony. While Beethoven's Fifth Symphony garners more attention, the Sixth is a masterpiece: five movements that take the listener through a gamut of emotions. From the awakening of cheerful feelings, through the peace of sitting by a brook, to the merriment of country folk, past thunder and storms, and ultimately to gratitude, the listener is captivated by the tone, texture and pacing of this masterpiece.

Like a great symphony, a great presentation is all about pacing. First of all, it is not a race. It is also not a quest to see how many words you can deliver in the shortest period of time. Often when people are under pressure, or get anxious (perhaps after seeing a yawn from the audience), they increase the speed of presentation.

You want to vary the pacing of your delivery: speed up some sections, draw out others. Perhaps most important, learn to pause.

Pause intentionally and comfortably. Stop talking. Make eye contact with the audience. Why?

The pause allows a key message to sink in. It also prepares the audience for an important message that is about to come.

There is power in the pause. In musical terms, this is called a rest. Rests are built into all musical scores, where their length varies from a whole rest (one beat) to fractions of a beat. Composers and conductors will often also write in breath marks (apostrophes) that instruct the wind instruments to take a breath and the non-wind instruments to take a slight pause. An even longer silent period is known as a caesura, indicated by two slash marks. This is a silent break in the music, the duration of which is dictated by the conductor.

Variety is the spice of life. So too is variety of pacing when you are championing your point of view.

#9. Add Interactivity

You can always begin a small to mid-sized talk by directly asking the audience why are they attending. Do this in a manner that thanks participants for being at the venue. "I'm honored that you folks have decided to give up part of your Saturday to be with me...So, tell me, what would you like to learn or accomplish in our time together?"

This opening provides the second advantage of getting to know your audience. You can modify your presentation to directly address some of the items brought up by the attendees. One word of caution: We've seen too many presenters, in response to audience inquiries, promise, "We'll cover that..." only to then disregard the input and fail to reference the concern in the talk. They instead just go ahead with their prepared remarks. This can result in negative feedback from the participant whose request was disregarded.

Your interactive exercise can be as simple as throwing a question out to the entire audience and asking individuals to respond. Or you can set up a dyad exercise. One that we frequently use as an example in our Enhance Your Presence training program is to ask participants to:

> "Think about a major change you have gone through in your personal or organizational life that you feel comfortable sharing. You will have two minutes to explain this story to the person next to you. As you tell your story, focus on the answer to two questions: What attitudes and behaviors served you well? What attitudes and behaviors got in your way? The role of the listener is to keep directing the speaker back to the answers to these questions. What attitudes and behaviors served the other person well, and what got in their way? I'll be telling you when we get close to the two-minute mark and then you will switch roles."

This exercise generates tremendous energy and audience participation. In fact, sometimes it is difficult to get the attendees to stop talking. At the end of the exercise when everyone has quieted down, we take an exaggerated pause until there is absolute silence in the room. As trainers, we share our observations and reflections; we ask audience members to do the same. The entire activity takes about ten minutes, and years later, these will be the ten minutes that participants are most likely to remember.

Another Type of Interactivity

Often, at the conclusion of a presentation, the audience is invited to ask questions, usually for a ten- to twenty-minute period. This is when you are interacting with the audience and vulnerable to a host of disparate audience motivations. Some attendees have questions related to clarification or expansion of a key point. Others will offer praise. These situations are easy to deal with. One of the most difficult types of question is the "gotcha." There are different varieties of this, but essentially, the audience member is trying to demonstrate his or her superior knowledge or viewpoint. Sometimes your inquisitor is even trying to embarrass you. Here are some tips to handle the gotchas:

- **Acknowledge the questioner.** Always make eye contact; breathe. Register that you have heard the other person. When in doubt—and to buy some additional time to compose your response—paraphrase the question, or ask for clarification. Then you can deliver or deflect in several ways.
- **If appropriate, thank the person.** They may have shed light on something you overlooked, or have an experience that is relevant. The questioner may have more recent data, or is personally involved in research on your topic. You can welcome their subject matter expertise. However, the stage is yours and so too is the microphone, so you should not provide them with an opportunity to grandstand. Politely thank them, then cut them off when they pause for breath.
- **Refocus their question.** People sometimes ramble on and have a hard time getting to the point and asking a question. Here's how you can handle this type of situation: "Thank you for raising this issue. I'm going to stop you there simply because it's a much larger discussion. Do you have a question related to what I presented?"

- **Deflect.** Acknowledge their point and pivot. One of the best ways to water down a vehemently opposing point of view is to say something like, "As you see from this gentleman's passionate response, this topic is sparking heated dialogue around the country/in our industry/in our community."
- **Mine the audience.** You can throw the controversy to the audience to recruit additional viewpoints; some may support yours, others may not. However, your willingness to be inclusive will win you big points with the audience.

#10. Use Humor, but Appropriately

Humor in a presentation is not about joking or delivering clown-like remarks. Rather, it comprises generally acceptable and timely statements that result in genuine laughter. Humor may be used early in a presentation to put the audience at ease and to relax you. This may often be achieved easily through some gentle self-deprecating remarks, an observation on a current event, or a reference to a funny remark made by an earlier presenter.

You can borrow liberally from pictures and jokes on the Internet to lighten the tone in the room. (Be aware of copyright issues; obtain permissions.) Clever remarks and visuals also allow you to drive home your points. For example, we've used a recent Internet posting to drive home the ambivalence that many women (and men) feel towards making health behavior change. The posting pointed to the bipolar nature of health advice in women's magazines: half of each issue is devoted to loving and accepting yourself just the way you are, while the other half is devoted to losing 20 pounds in three weeks!

To be successful, humor must be well-timed. Comedians follow a tested format. They employ a set-up that engages the audience's attention and follow up with the punch line. Set-up, punch line. Set-up, punch line. Great comedians keep both as short as possible. Consider Henny Youngman, whose best known one liner was, "Take my wife....please!"

#11. Roll with the Punches

No matter how well you prepare, there will be unexpected challenges. The microphone screeches; the projector fails to work; there's a loud noise or periodic laughter emanating from the adjacent room. Breathe deeply. Go with the flow. Say something lighthearted. A squeaking noise coming from the ceiling? "Well, that must be the NSA grabbing our metadata." A thumping noise from the speakers? A great time to practice tap dancing. A broken projector and no slides? An opportunity to roll up your sleeves and ask the audience to share their experiences. You go from being a presenter to acting more as a facilitator and commentator. Here's an example of how Mark did this during a presentation:

> "One of my most impactful presentations took place during a daytime session in which, right before I was to begin, we lost electricity. So, no slides. The subject of my talk was on stress management. I had the group rearrange their chairs to sit in a circle and I then posed this question: 'Each of you has a technique you use to deal with stress and change. Tell us what works for you.' I then used each person's answers as the jumping-off point to further discuss and elaborate upon their contributions."

#12. Take Every Opportunity to Speak and to Improve

When starting out, take advantage of every opportunity to speak to groups. Hold open houses at your facility; speak to religious and civic organizations. Hone your message. After each presentation, honestly critique how you did. Remember, you will be your harshest judge. If you have the opportunity to video your talk, use this for reference. What did you do well? In what areas could you improve? How well did you listen to, para-phrase, and answer participant's questions? Were there some awkward moments or stumbles? How might you overcome this the next time you present? Try using the following checklist. On a scale from 1 to 10, with 10 being best, how would you rate your:

- ☐ Pacing and timing
- ☐ Voice quality
- ☐ Understandability of message
- ☐ Audiovisuals
- ☐ Emphasis of key points
- ☐ Ability to clarify your remarks when necessary
- ☐ Effectiveness in providing an emotional experience
- ☐ Introduction
- ☐ Conclusion
- ☐ Answering audience member's questions
- ☐ Ability to hold the audience's attention
- ☐ Storytelling
- ☐ Voice quality
- ☐ Level of interactivity

Use this checklist to prepare thoroughly to improve the content and delivery of your talk. Furthermore, rehearsing and getting feedback will also help you feel more confident and calm when it's time to officially deliver the presentation. It's one step towards overcoming presentation anxiety. The fear of speaking is a complex experience. In fact, it's such an omnipresent and important topic that we've dedicated the next chapter to it.

Want the "Cheat Sheet"?

We've put all the major presentation tips into a one-page flowchart. You can use it both as a guide and a checklist. Download the *Enhance Your Presence* Flowchart free at:

bit.do/changewell

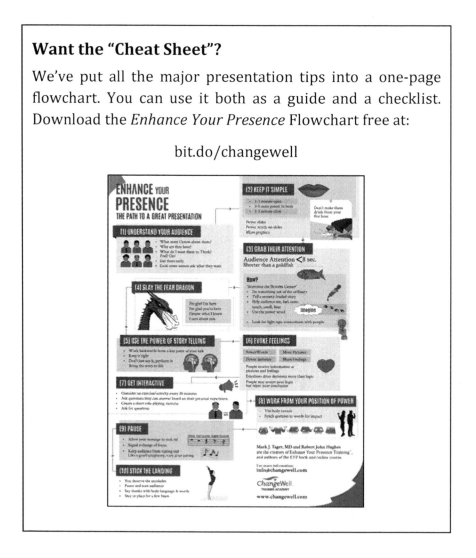

Chapter 5

Slay The Fear Dragon

"The great thing then, in all education, is to make our nervous system our ally as opposed to our enemy."
—William James

Imagine a tropical jungle. It is nighttime. The air is hot, heavy, oppressive. Ahead of us we see flickering fires and we hear chanting voices and throbbing drums. As we approach, the outline of a tall stone structure appears. It is a pyramid with a high open platform surrounded by torches. A group of bare-chested men in warrior dress appear on the platform, leading another figure clad in a white robe. The crowd erupts into a frenzy. We focus in on the figure and realize that it's you. Yes, dear reader, you are atop the pyramid surrounded by blazing torches. The question is: *Who are you? Are you the next monarch? Or are you the next sacrifice?*

As you can imagine, all of your bodily senses are going crazy. Your pulse rate is soaring, your breathing is shallow and panicky, you may feel sick to your stomach, light-headed, full of fear.

This is precisely how some people feel when they confront the prospect of speaking before a group of people: terrified.

On a slow news day, editors trot out one of those 'Top 10" stories. You've probably seen the one that rates "fear of public speaking" as the # 1 phobia, ahead of spiders, snakes, being trapped in a tiny space, etc. Jerry Seinfeld has a well-known joke that suggests that if we're attending a funeral, some of us would prefer to be the guy in the coffin rather than the person giving the eulogy. Yes, some people feel they would rather die than talk to a group of people.

We have perfected a process in our *EYP* workshop that directly addresses presentation anxiety. In about an hour, we are able to dispel the fear completely, or at least reduce it to a point where it can be comfortably managed.

Our process begins with the definition of anxiety:

> *a feeling of worry, nervousness, or unease, typically about an imminent event or something with an uncertain outcome.*[46]

The first phrase we confront is "feeling of worry, nervousness or unease." Let's deal with unease first. What most people mean by a "bad feeling" is a combination of physical sensations combined with an interpretation that the sensations indicate something bad is happening. The problem is that the human body—wonderful machine that it is—has only a few ways to respond to stress, and disregards whether that stress is perceived as "positive" or "negative."[47]

If we meet someone to whom we are intensely attracted, we experience an increase in heart rate; our breathing changes; we perspire; we feel light-headed; we have "butterflies" in our stomach. The odd thing is that when we are frightened, we may experience most, if not all, of the same physical symptoms. But what is different is the interpretation. Under one circumstance those physical sensations are exciting, delightful, and signify to us that we have met someone extraordinary. But under another circumstance, the identical sensations are terrifying and their meaning is clear: we are in big trouble. How do we know? We FEEL it. And the feeling is one of "unease."

Here's the fact: feelings can only tell us what we're feeling. They do not tell us what it means. A sunny day with blue skies and a breeze is a beautiful day unless you happen to be farmer standing in a field of drought-stricken plants. It's not the physical facts that make it beautiful or terrible—it's the context and interpretation. Likewise, it's not the pulse rate or perspiration that tells us "I'm afraid," because those same symptoms may also be present when we've just fallen in love. The same set of symptoms inside a different interpretation has us feel alive and empowered. If we shift the way we interpret our feelings, we gain power over the physical.

Our recommendation: think of anxiety as one side of a coin. The other side is energy. When you feel afraid, anxious or worried about the outcome of a presentation, flip the coin over. Tap into the energy that rises from the physical symptoms. Instead of telling yourself "I'm scared," you might try saying: "I notice my heart rate is up, my breathing is more rapid. I'm taking in more oxygen and distributing it throughout my body. My energy is building. My body is preparing me for an outstanding performance by waking up all my senses. I'm EXCITED!"

That handles the word "feeling." The next part of the definition is "worry or nervousness." Let's take you back to the top of that jungle pyramid. If it's clear you will not be harmed and instead your job is simply to give a speech, do you feel better now?

Most people would say "no." They will have their attention on the outcome and because of that they will experience a great deal of pressure. How well will I perform? Will they like what I say? Do they like me? etc.

In our workshop, we ask our participants, "When you step out on the stage, who is the hero?" It looks like it's you—the speaker. After all, you're the one in the spotlight. It's easy to conclude it's all up to you. But what if that's not true at all? What if it's actually all up to the audience? **What if the audience is the hero?** You have the message, but they have the power to do something with it. Your job is to deliver the message as capably as you can. Their job is to listen and then do what they think is appropriate. They may run right out and do what you say. Or not.

For sure, it would probably be better if they took your advice. But realistically, how likely is that? This shift alone reduces the pressure to perform. Instead of you being expected to "save the world," all you have to do is give a talk. Give your talk as a gift from the heart, a service to humanity. You can do that, right?

Perhaps you're still worried about the outcome. But what percent of the time do things turn out the way you want? It's a trick question because the answer is hardly reassuring.

The most successful career hitter in baseball is Ty Cobb, who holds the record for the highest career batting average with .367. As you probably know, that means Ty Cobb succeeded in hitting the baseball only one time out of every three, and failed to get a hit 63% of the time.

In what business is a 63% failure rate acceptable? Answer: Just about any business you can imagine! A success rate of 36% sustained over a career is an extraordinary accomplishment. We know a few really good sales executives. Their new business "closing ratio" is around 15-20%. That means they close two of every ten presentations. At ChangeWell, we send out e-mails and are excited when our open rate gets up close to 20%. That's good. But it means 80% of the people who got our e-mail did not read it. Most people don't realize how thoroughly the odds appear to be stacked against their success. We say there is a more realistic way to measure success.

The truth is that things mostly do not turn out how we would like, but they always turn out the way they turn out. They may love your talk. They may not. What's likely is that 80% of the audience will walk out of the room without any memory at all of what you said. 20% will remember a fraction of what you said—for maybe 24 hours. Then they will forget also. So judging your success by the outcome of one presentation is hardly empowering.

But even after all this re-contextualizing, we still don't feel comfortable. And in a way, it's funny! I mean—*they asked you to speak, right? They may even be paying you to speak.* In so many ways, you've won even before you walk out on stage.

While that may be comforting, maybe what we need is a bigger game. Like Ty Cobb, welcome every at-bat. Intend to swing for the fences. And having done the best we can do, humbly accept the result.

You want to play the biggest of all possible games. What's possible, but not guaranteed, is that your talk may touch a single individual who turns out to be the next Oprah Winfrey. What you say may change a life forever. You may never know that you had that kind of impact. You may never be acknowledged. But your message could be the single pebble that triggers an avalanche of change. If that's the likely outcome, would you take the stage and endeavor to do your very best every time? Most people we know say: "Yes, of course." Take the stage with the intention of changing the world—and you just might.

Nervous Energy vs. Nerves

Hopefully, you now have a better handle on how to distinguish nervous energy—which can be channeled—from anxiety and fear—to intention and confidence.

Thirty years ago, Mark learned a technique to help him channel his nervous energy, and slay the fear dragon. He's been using it ever since. Here is his story.

> "In 1984 I had written a book entitled *Working Well* with Marjorie Blanchard, CEO of Blanchard Training. Her husband, Ken Blanchard, is most well known for his series of *One Minute Manager* books. Margie and I coined the term "bad bosses" and enumerated the handful of behaviors that set employees up for poor productivity and illness. We also identified health- and productivity-promoting behaviors.
>
> I was in my early 30s and I was chosen to give a talk on Leadership, Health, and Productivity to the Young Presidents' Organization, more commonly known as the YPO. If you're not familiar with this organization, it's the Who's Who of International Industry—each YPO member had to be a CEO running a multi-million dollar company, all before reaching the tender age of 40.

So, there I was...a somewhat naïve, health-promoting doctor running a fledgling company with—at the time—five employees...and I was going to talk to the captains of industry about leading well.

I was so nervous....no, I was scared. And I remember when Ken Blanchard, probably noticing my ashen appearance, shared a four-sentence 'mantra.' He told me I could use it to focus my attention and lose the fear. It went like this:

I'm glad I'm here

I'm glad you're here

I know what I know, and

I care about you."

Let's break each sentence down.

I'm glad I'm here. This first sentence helps to set tone and demeanor. It is the best way to transfer nervous energy into a sense of potential enjoyment. You can't genuinely say, "I'm glad I'm here," without smiling.

I'm glad you're here. This phrase should reflect the feeling and sense that you are honored to be in a position to share your knowledge and experience. Attendees have honored you with the gift of their time and now it's up to you to use it well. And again, every time you say to yourself that you are "glad," what do you subconsciously do? ...Right, you smile.

I know what I know. This phrase addresses what may be the biggest hurdle, particularly for analytical and data-driven professionals. We have been trained in a competitive system that rank-orders and judges individuals by how much they know. Unless you ARE the world's expert on a given subject, chances are there will be people sitting in the audience who know more about your subject than you do...or who just read the latest literature that came out yesterday. It's easy to be flooded by feelings of inadequacy if you sense that you will be harshly judged. Here's the antidote to this mental poison. You are the only person on the planet with your unique synthesis of attitude, knowledge, point of view and experience on any given subject. This makes you an expert in knowing what you know. Others have a different set—but yours is valid and perfect. So let it rip.

The last sentence should also provide guidance on how you conduct your program.

I care about you. This means that you won't "should" on your audience. You won't bludgeon them with "you must," "you have to," "I want you to." It also means you won't bore them: you'll be sensitive to clues of restlessness and plan breaks accordingly. You'll attend to their reactions: when you see a few yawns, engage them in an activity. Most of all it means your intention is to serve them with a message that makes life better.

Mark has said these four phrases to himself hundreds of times since that fateful day in the mid-80s. If it works for you to borrow these phrases—go for it.

The Sarnoff Squeeze

Only recently did we learn that this mantra originated with Dorothy Sarnoff, an opera singer who became a famous presentation coach. She had a role in the Broadway production of *The King and I* that starred Yul Brynner. One night she found him backstage pushing with all his might against a wall. She asked him what he was doing. He told her that the exertion calmed him down.[48]

Dorothy experimented and eventually developed "The Sarnoff Squeeze." Here's how it works:

- You stand or sit comfortably.

- Slowly breathe in.

- As you are about to breathe out, contract your abs—the "six pack" of muscles in your mid-section.

- While you continue to squeeze, exhale slowly and steadily.

- Repeat this a few more times—until you feel more relaxed and focused.

Create Your Own Pre-Presentation Rituals

There are some other rituals that you can include in your preparation to stem presentation anxiety. One set of them goes back some 2,000 years.

Imagine that you had to step into a fighting ring, naked except for a loincloth. Standing across from you is a 300-pound behemoth of a man whose piercing eyes tell you that he will only be satisfied when you are thrown out of the ring.

Welcome to the ancient art of Sumo.

Everyone is familiar with the Japanese national sport of sumo wrestling, an athletic practice that goes back centuries. Far fewer people have seen a sumo bout from start to finish. In a sumo-wrestling bout, the two wrestlers are locked in an intense battle to push each other out of the ring. Many sumo matches are decided in only a matter of seconds.

Although the match itself may take only a few seconds, the pre-match rituals for the fighters last far longer. Sumo is intimately entwined with ancient Shinto ritual, and sumo wrestlers perform an elaborate set of rituals before they begin their match. One of the most visible rituals, and one that immediately precedes the bout itself, is a foot-stomping ritual. Each sumo wrestler will lift one leg high in the air, then stomp it down, before performing the same action with the other leg. Only then are the sumo wrestlers ready to face each other in combat.

This leg-stomping ritual has long been considered a traditional practice—derived from Shintoism—to scare away demons before a match. In this ritual, we see a centuries-long affirmation of the importance of grounding and centering oneself before an event that requires full concentration and focus.

Western audiences often under-appreciate the athleticism and challenge of sumo wrestling; in reality, it is one of the most intensely confrontational sports currently practiced. If a sumo wrestler is not fully present in the moment, he has already lost. As he stomps his feet on the hard-packed dirt of the ring, surrounded by thousands of spectators and only several feet away from his antagonist, the sumo wrestler grounds himself in the moment with this ancient ritual.

To benefit from this eons-long piece of sumo wisdom, you do not need to don a loincloth or wear your hair in a top-knot. All you need is to stomp your feet, one at a time, as a pre-presentation ritual. Upon taking the stage, plant your feet and feel the swell of energy RISE from the ground to the soles of your feet and up your legs, magnetically connecting you to solid ground.

Mobilize Your Energy

There are other "whole body" exercises that can relax you and get your energy flowing smoothly and visibly for all to see. Visit the Chinatown section of any major US city (or go to China for that matter) and, in the mornings, you will see a collection of usually elderly Chinese women and men gathering for Tai Chi. While learning the classic 108 movements takes hours of study and practice, the warm-up exercises for the class can be mastered by anyone. Short instructional videos can readily be found online. These warm-up exercises (Fig. 8 & 9) are designed to get your "chi" (energy) flowing. The first involves twisting at the waist in both directions.

Fig. 8

In the second, you sweep your arms down as if throwing something behind you.

Fig. 9

Attend to the Basics

There are also some less esoteric activities you should do before and during your presentation. These include:

- **Go to the bathroom before you go on stage.** This one is pretty basic, but it is amazing how a full bladder will speed up your delivery—to the detriment of audience comprehension.
- **Drink hot water with lemon and honey.** This old "hot toddy" recipe works well for the common cold (minus the alcohol). Even if you aren't sick, sipping this before going on stage can sooth your vocal chords.
- **Use throat lozenges.** In the course of a longer presentation, your throat gets dry and it's easy to lose the power of your voice. Suck a non-menthol lozenge during breaks in the program. (Mark is a fan of Burt's Bees® Natural Throat Drops)
- **Time your eating.** Having too much food in your stomach can redirect blood flow to your gut and cause you to feel and act sluggish. It is probably best to refrain from eating for about two hours before a presentation. If you feel that you need some food in your stomach, eat a small portion of something light and easily digestible.
- **Wash your hands under hot water.** Have you ever noticed how people who apply for jobs have cold, clammy hands? It's the fight or flight response in action. You can help calm your nervous system by washing your hands in hot water before getting on stage—and combine this with a few deep breaths.
- **Bring room temperature water on stage.** Certainly a must. Cold water tightens your throat.

- **Consider the backdrop when you dress.** It's a good idea to find out in advance what color backdrop you will be speaking in front of. Dress to create some contrast so you can be seen more easily and your movements and gestures can have more impact. A dark blue suit is nice, but if you are in front of a dark black background, you may be camouflaged.
- **Play your song in your head.** Each of us has our power song. You can play it in your head before you walk up to the podium. For Robert, it's "Start Me Up" by the Rolling Stones. For Mark, it's the opening of the third movement of Brahms' Piano Concerto No. 1 in D Minor. To each his own.

Don't Become a Self-Fulfilling Prophecy: Stick the Landing

We have seen hundreds of speakers deliver a better than decent presentation, right up until the end. Then, as they leave the stage, they roll their eyes, or shrug, or laugh to themselves, or make faces at a friend in the crowd. The speaker actions seem to say: "Yeah, I know, I'm not that good. But what did you expect. Hey, I tried, OK?"

After seeing dozens of presenters behaving this way, we asked ourselves why.

We call these "self-dismissive gestures." This kind of body language at the end of a presentation is actually very understandable. It is a plea for sympathy, from the audience. "I know I wasn't good. Please don't judge me harshly, OK?" This feeling springs from the deepest well of human insecurity. We are sometimes secretly afraid that we are never enough. Rather than wait for the world to deliver that verdict, we try to soften the blow by claiming defeat.

When you send out the signal that "I am not taking my own presentation seriously," it sets the stage for a self-fulfilling prophecy. Remember what we said in Chapter 2 about tone of voice, gestures, and body language. These need to be coherent with the presentation. When you deliver a world-changing message, but end with defeated body language, your actions undermine your message. People will see your self-dismissive ending as license to forget what you told them.

If you want people to leave your presentation with the feeling that they must remember what you taught, be sure to "stick the landing." We take this metaphor from the performances of world-class gymnasts. At the end of their routine, they finish big and arrive at a triumphant posture, with arms raised and a victorious smile. It may have taken a hop or wiggle to get there, but they act as if their performance was worth a gold medal. Once their routine ends they have done all they can do. They know the rest is up to the judges.

That's how it is with your talk. As we said earlier, your job is not to change the world. Your job is to deliver your message. When you come to the end of your talk, "stick the landing" means you act as if you have succeeded.

It's the audience's job to change the world. They are the hero. After your presentation—it's up to them.

For most of us, performing is unfamiliar. So we hold back. Been to a karaoke bar? Do you remember the really accomplished almost professional singers? Probably not. You probably don't remember the truly mediocre efforts either. We only remember the ones who grab the bull by the horns, enthusiastically put embarrassment aside, and commit to the tune. At the end of the song, no apologies will be necessary, because there is nothing to apologize for. No self-dismissive signals are warranted, because there is nothing to dismiss. You did your best and had fun doing it.

One of Robert's coaches observed him in a practice session giving a very tight, conservative, and risk free presentation. It was professional, proficient, and really boring. No passion. She interrupted and asked, "If you knew this was the last time you would ever get to speak to these people, would you be speaking this way?" Robert had to concede the point. He realized, "If this is my last time on stage, I want to go out with no regrets." If that's how you feel, let it rip. Go for the gold and be sure to stick the landing.

How to Stick the Landing

- **Bring your presentation full circle**. The end should relate to the beginning providing a sense of closure. Neuroscience provides an even more compelling reason. As we said in Chapter 2, people are most likely to remember what you said first—and last. Put your key point up front. Circle back to it at the end. If you opened a talk on world hunger with a story about a woman in an African village, revisit her story at the end. Use the power of the story to get attention and hold it. Come back to the story to show how your message could make a difference.

- **Return to your position of power...and wait there**. All too often presenters adopt the "gosh, golly, aw shucks" posture. Instead, return to a position of power with head held high, chest up, back straight, hands in a comfortable position. When you get there, hold it for a count of five, or even longer, if applause continues.

- **Acknowledge the audience.** Use words, gestures and body language to thank them for their time and generous attention. Acknowledgments vary according to audience size, allotted time, theme, and culture. Your acknowledgment can be a full horizontal audience scan, a genuine smile, and eye contact with those with whom you have connected. It can be a simple nod or two of the head, a mouthed "thank you" or a wave of the hand. Whatever technique you use, make certain to take your time.

- **Shift your perspective.** If this is hard for you because you don't think you deserve it, make a mental shift. The applause is for your message and how it made them feel. You are the representative of your message. On behalf of the message itself, show your gratitude to your audience. The greatest performers in the world take it even deeper. What you did caused the audience to think, feel, and become inspired. It's thrilling for a human being to feel that way. The truth is: They are actually applauding themselves. Honor them with your presence and your thanks. Employ the technique long enough for you to feel uncomfortable—and then keep doing it just a bit longer. Remember, these are the people you hope will take your message and do something with it.

- **End on an inspirational note.** Motivational sayings affixed to evocative images seem to dominate our email box and the social media sites we are part of. There is a certain power to a well-chosen quotation accompanied by an appropriate image. When you use a motivational quote to conclude a presentation, you have the opportunity to bring to bear all your theatrical skills to end on a memorable note. The quote can be intensely powerful if you read it in such a way that your pacing, intonation, inflection, and emphasis accurately reflect the intention of the writer.

As an example, let's take a look at a quote we often use to close our presentations and trainings on *Building Resilience,* a popular training program that has been used globally in corporations and organizations for the last twenty-five years. *Building Resilience* teaches a set of skills based upon an integrated model that helps recipients get stronger to meet the ever-increasing challenges of life and work. The philosophy of the program and the Resilience Model, based upon a unique temperament-based assessment, the PowerSource Profile, are described in Mark's book, *Transforming Stress into Power* (ChangeWell Publishing).

To end a *Building Resilience* program on a high note, we will often quote Phillips Brooks, an American Episcopal clergyman and author from Boston. Brooks was an outspoken opponent of slavery during the Civil War, and was no stranger to the strength needed to take on noble, difficult challenges. His remarks are as timely today as they were in the early 1860s. They make a fitting ending for this chapter:

"Make the best use of what is in your power, and take the rest as it happens. Do not pray for easy lives. Pray to be a stronger person. Do not pray for tasks equal to your powers. Pray for powers equal to your tasks. Then the doing of your work shall be no miracle, but you shall be the miracle."

Want to Spice Up Your Presentations?

Interspersing selected motivational quotes can help you maintain audience attention. It can also allow you to end your presentation on a high note. We've prepared a baker's dozen PowerPoint slides with our favorite quotes, some of them drawn from the pages of this book. To get your free set of motivational quotes, go to:

bit.do/changewell

Chapter 6

Tap Into Your Passion

*"All the forces in the world are not so powerful
as an idea whose time has come."*
—Victor Hugo

This quote comes from one of France's greatest writers, the author of *Les Misérables* and the work Americans know as The Hunchback of Notre Dame. His country honored him by placing his picture on a banknote and with a prominent burial place in the Pantheon, overlooking the city of Paris. Theater and movie audiences have thrilled to Hugo's vision of the French Revolution and the struggle of French peasants to gain freedom.

It was a struggle marked by tragedy, towering emotions, and fiery passions, all organized around an idea: Liberty, Equality, Fraternity. Today that phrase is the motto of France.

Such is the power of ideas.

Ideas do not live outside of human beings. Ideas are like a virus. We are their hosts. and we spread them.

When the idea, as a virus, spreads far enough and wide enough, there is an outbreak of epidemic proportions and the idea becomes the new reality. The French Revolution changed the course of history by triggering the global decline of absolute monarchies, replacing them with republics and liberal democracies.

Thomas Paine, one of America's founding fathers, wrote, "An army of principles will penetrate where an army of soldiers cannot. Neither the Channel nor the Rhine will arrest its progress. It will march on the horizon of the world and it will conquer."

This chapter is about how that happens.

In the Vietnam era, a popular anti-war slogan was: "What if they gave a war and nobody came." The slogan points to a central truth about ideas. The biggest enemy of an idea is not the opposition to an idea, no matter how fierce—it's apathy. If no one cares about your idea, it's dead. In order for your idea to spread, people have to care about it. And the first person who should care about it is you. The way you demonstrate that you care about an idea is you take a stand for it and express it. You speak with passion and the intention to pass your idea along, have it take hold in another human being, and ignite their passion.

What makes a speaker "great?" In our workshop, we hear things like this:

- "He was enthusiastic."
- "She was convincing."
- "His energy was infectious."
- "She was talking right to me as if she knew me."
- "He was really eloquent, organized."

- "He made it look effortless."

- "She was passionate about the subject."

- "He inspired me."

The Latin roots of the word "inspire" mean "to breathe into." The word itself means: "To fill someone with the urge or ability to do or feel something." Synonyms include: stimulate, motivate, encourage, influence, rouse, move, stir, energize, galvanize, and incite.

Participants who come into our workshop feel they would like to have these qualities—but some have a long way to go. We've been asked: "What can I do to get 'fired up?' How do I do it so I don't come off like a huckster jackass?" In other words, what is the access road to a naturally animated and authentic sense of passion? How do we tap into the source of that energy?

Exercising Your Passion

We developed an exercise that takes only a couple of minutes but shocks people into a different way of thinking about themselves. We introduce the subject of speaking with passion and "tapping into your own natural charisma."

We teach the distinction from the front of the room, classroom-style, but only briefly. We then direct an exercise that will be videotaped and critiqued. To raise the stakes even higher, we allow no time at all for preparation. We simply announce the topic, and tell participants to "go."

The results are miraculous. At the end of their talk nearly everyone is surprised and delighted by their own performance. They are even more surprised when the group gives them positive feedback. Participants whose previous talks had been marked by lame language artifacts like "umm," "ahh," "like," "y'know," suddenly become organized, eloquent, and persuasive. It is as if a being unknown to them had suddenly taken command of their body, heart, mind, and voice.

What is the secret behind results like this? It's the topic. "Deliver a one-minute talk about something you *believe*. GO!"

Even the most timid, fearful speakers become noticeably more confident, passionate, and inspirational. They are stunned that they could deliver a talk this well received *with no preparation at all.*

If the speaker has experience and has mastered some presentation techniques, the talk can border on the extraordinary. But even participants who insist "I'll never be very good" discover within themselves a power they never knew they had.

It's the often-untapped power of passionate expression.

One of our workshop participants, a top corporate trainer for a major technology company, told us that this exercise completely destroyed his fear-based belief that he needed to elaborately prepare for every talk. For the first time, he experienced a type of eloquence and persuasion that shocked him so much it altered his own view of his competence as a speaker. He realized that the source of his power is what comes from his heart. One of the oldest slogans of corporate sales trainers applies here: "Enthusiasm ends with the letter I, A, S, M which stands for 'I Am Sold Myself.'" We hate clichés, but sometimes the truth behind them is inescapable.

In order to be passionate about something, you must believe in it. If you are "sold yourself," that means you have welcomed the idea into your being, you have incubated it like a virus, and now you are ready to spread it. And that will require enough energy to transmit it so that it takes root and spreads. As it spreads far and wide, your idea will become disconnected from you. Others will think it was their idea and they will spread it. When the idea has spread to enough people, it becomes the new reality. This is how you make an idea's time come. This is how you change the world.

This is the secret behind the greatest speeches in history. Martin Luther King Jr. said: "I have a dream." He described a world where people of every race lived together in harmony. It was not yet a reality. But it was a real possibility. People who hear him speak find themselves touched by his words and inspired by the possibility he declared.

When you are in the presence of a possibility you have created, you may find that it begins to reframe your life in a way that brings new energy and meaning to everyday living. You are giving your life to bring that possibility into being. It's a choice that can bring energy and passion into your life. That makes you a leader. People will follow you because when they hear you speak, you seem to be saying what is already in their hearts. This is why we say:

"If you believe in a possibility for others and you present it with passion, no one can resist you."

Passion is the fertilizer of possibility. Power is derived from passionately expressing a possibility that you see not for yourself but for all people. For example, if you were to say "I see the possibility that everyone in the world could have free abundant energy." No one can debate that you see that. Others might debate that it's impractical, illogical, and undesirable, but they can't negate a belief, opinion, or vision.

Now if you can develop a case for that idea and you express that case with passion, it becomes very hard to refute you. Every attempt to refute your vision actually adds weight, substance, and persistence to the vision, sustaining it and increasing it. As we said at the start of this chapter, the mortal enemy of an idea is not the people and forces opposed to it; the biggest enemy is apathy.

Within, or just previous to, our lifetimes, a whole lot of things have happened that were once considered to be unlikely or impossible: the vote for women; the success of the civil rights movement; and the legalization of gay marriage. These were all ideas that were unthinkable at a certain time. There was powerful, sometimes violent opposition. But enough people got behind them and when they reached a tipping point, those ideas became the new and inevitable reality. Looking back, it seems like a normal, evolutionary process.

How to Structure a Persuasive Talk

Enough theory. How can you structure a talk so that you maximize the potential to persuade?

Nancy Duarte is a presentation expert who worked with Al Gore on the slide show that became the basis for Gore's Oscar-winning film on climate change, *An Inconvenient Truth.* Duarte has uncovered what she calls "The Secret Structure of Great Talks." She presents her findings in one of the most-watched TED Talks of all time. We encourage you to view it:

https://www.ted.com/talks/nancy_duarte_the_secret_structure_of_great_talks

Duarte says that the greatest speeches of all time follow an unusual structure. Here is the diagram:

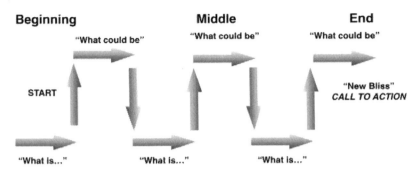

Graphic Adapted from *Harvard Business Review*[49]

Here's our summary of the formula:

1. Make your talk about "Today's status quo vs. the new reality or possibility."
2. Structure your talk into sections where you compare "what is" with "what could be."
3. Use vivid, emotionally appealing imagery and language.
4. Include the arguments against your idea as part of "what is."
5. Contrast those arguments with the new reality.
6. End with a compelling picture of "the new reality" fully realized and invite your audience to take action.

Let the power of your beliefs have you speak up—and speak out. Let your ideas loose in the world. Addressing the 2005 graduating class at Stanford, Steve Jobs said:

"Remembering you are going to die is the best way I know to avoid the trap of thinking you have something to lose. You are already naked. There is no reason not to follow your heart."

Chapter 7

Hone Your Story Telling

*"Tell me the facts and I'll learn. Tell me the truth and I'll believe.
But tell me a story and it will live in my heart forever."*
—Native American Proverb

What are the elements of a great story? And why should you tell one? Increasingly, science is documenting the compelling attributes of a well-told story, as a way to engage audience attention and to ensure that your message will be remembered. We believe:

Attention is the filtration system of the human consciousness.

The challenge, of course, is that the recipients of our words have a head full of swirling images, and they are usually already at cognitive overload when their butts are sitting in the seats in front of us.

147

Cognitive Load Theory, a theory of cognitive psychology first developed by Professor John Sweller in the 1980s, is an instructive theory to apply here.[50] We can think of cognitive load as the mental space that new information occupies in a person's brain. If the brain is required to handle too much complex information—if the cognitive load is greater than the listener's capacity—the information simply will not stick.

Today, business professionals are being asked to process more and more complicated data and facts. With our ever-connected existence, there is no escape from the constant stream of information. Audience members could be halfway across the world from their office, but they are still checking their e-mail, watching the stock market, and Skyping their colleagues. When you present, you are competing with all these demands on peoples' attention, demands that they consider to be just as important and urgent as anything you have to say. To put it another way, their capacity to handle new information is low. As the presenter, you must reduce the cognitive load of your presented information to maximize the ability of your audience members to absorb it.

But how? To understand this, we must first break down the three types of cognitive load. **Intrinsic cognitive load** is the amount of load imposed by the learning task. This type of load is correlated with the characteristics of the information itself. The more difficult or complex the subject matter, the greater the intrinsic cognitive load. **Germane cognitive load** refers to the way the information is processed. Is information interpreted, classified, inferred, differentiated?[51] **Extraneous cognitive load** has to do with how information is presented.

These three types of cognitive loads combine to comprise the **sum cognitive load**, the full amount of stress that a presentation places on the engine that is the brain. Lessen the cognitive load, lessen the stress, and you will help ensure that your information is absorbed. Of the three types of cognitive load, it is extraneous cognitive load that is most malleable. We cannot change the information itself, we cannot change the way it needs to be processed (not fully, at least), but we can change the way that information is *presented*.

Your presentation must reduce the complexity of the information, while tapping into the way that people naturally learn information.

This is where the ancient art of storytelling comes in.

Light up More of their Brains

Only recently have scientists begun to document—through studies involving fMRI—storytelling's power to strongly imprint vivid memories in people's minds.

Research has uncovered how the spoken presentation of information will activate two areas of the brain: Broca's area and Wernicke's area. These areas are concerned with the production and comprehension, respectively, of language. When we speak in words and numbers—as we do most of the time, in daily life—these are the areas of the brain that are receiving our spoken signal. Effective storytelling, on the other hand, activates as many as *seven* areas of the brain.[52]

These areas include the motor cortex, responsible for coordinating physical movement; the olfactory cortex, responsible for smells; the visual cortex, responsible for sight; and the auditory cortex, responsible for sound (Fig. 11).

149

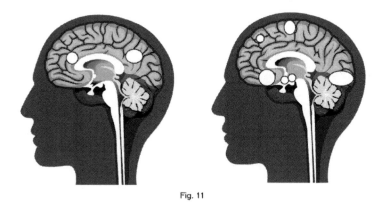

Fig. 11

Spoken information activates two areas of the brain, effective story telling
activates as many as seven.

Examining this illustration of brain areas, you may start to realize: a good story brings the listener along with it, causing the brain to experience the described sensations as if the listener himself is a participant in the story. The power of these sensory associations with the story makes the information more comprehensible, and more memorable.

Similarly, a story creates an emotional connection with the listener. Just as a good story excites the sensory regions of the brain, so does a good story invite the listener to share in the emotions of the characters. As Paul J. Zak, the pioneer in the field of neuroeconomics, describes it: "character-driven stories with emotional content result in a better understanding of the key points a speaker wishes to make and enable better recall of these points weeks later. In terms of making [an] impact, this blows the standard PowerPoint presentation to bits."[53]

Thus, neuroscience has been confirming what seasoned actors and orators have known for centuries.

A good story is better remembered, and more persuasive, than a simple recitation of facts.

Let's look at what comprises an effective story. Here is one told by Ron Hartley, a participant in one of our workshops.

"My father was a magician.

No, it wasn't his occupation, but when I was a young boy he enjoyed performing at church socials and community events. As you know, magicians need assistants, sometimes the unseen kind. As a young boy, I often had the assignment of helping rabbits magically appear from the hat—Abe Lincoln style—that was set on a table with a concealed hole.

I would hide under the table prior to the show with the little box of live bunnies (spoiler alert) and would feed them up through the hat when it was placed on the hole and the false bottom opened up. There were audible clues given by Dad as to when I should present the bunny to be grabbed by the ears and magically lifted out.

I remember one time I was holding up a rabbit, but I didn't think it was time yet to let it go. It felt to me like the little guy was trying to grab the edge of the hole with his front feet and pull himself out, so I held on tightly. In reality, my father was on the other side tugging on the ears trying to extract the little guy. For a few seconds the tug of war went on until I realized what was happening. I quickly released him and the crowd cheered as the bunny emerged—a few inches longer than when he started.

Do you ever feel like that little rabbit—unsure of what lies ahead and pulled in a couple of different directions? Sometimes you just need to let go and watch the magic happen."

This is a short story—only 130 words. To present it to a crowd would take only a couple of minutes. Yet its impact far outstrips its size. Let's explore why this story is so powerful.

1. Begin with the end in mind. From the standpoint of presence, your story must have a point. And that point should be for the benefit of your audience, not for yourself. We've all been exposed to certain politicians who tell stories, the whole purpose of which is to make them look great. You want the audience to be the hero.

So figure out what particular point you want to make. In this case, the story illustrated a key point in stress and life management. Namely, the importance of letting go. Then work backwards to develop your story.

2. Evoke emotions. Make them universal ones, at that. Here we have a father-son bonding story. This can certainly trigger feelings in the audience.

3. Engage the senses. We can easily relate to, even feel, the pressure of being cramped in a small box beneath the stage. Our hands experience the sinews of the kicking rabbit. It's easy to imagine the smells that radiate from nervous rabbits in a confined space. And anyone who has ever seen a magic act immediately flashes to mind the rich, vibrant colors worn by the magician and any props or lighting.

4. Generate tension. A humorous story about a magician and his assistant son is not a nail-biter, of course, but we remain gripped to the story because we recognize the conflict—in this case, a literal tug-of-war, with potentially embarrassing effects.

If we want attention from the crowd, we need tension in the story.[54]

Closely related to the subject of tension is that of suspense: not knowing what's going to happen next. This anticipation has been shown in studies as a time-lag phenomenon. This skill is one that is employed by every good comedian. It is the lag, the down-moment, before the reveal or the punch line. In the telling of the story, you want to build appropriate anticipation, through pauses. Give yourself permission to set the tone in a dramatic fashion. Use one or more of the techniques that we've described earlier, such as the eyedropper, or feel free to exaggerate the pauses.

5. Come full circle. The story opens with a hook, clearly describes what takes place, and ends on a motivational, inspirational message. Nice and tight; we are left with a feeling of completeness.

Remember that it takes time to "own" a story. It will improve with the telling, particularly as you have opportunities to observe the audience's reaction and modify your tale.

From Bunny Rabbits to Racehorses

The Austrian endocrinologist, Dr. Hans Selye, is widely regarded as the father of the field of stress research. Pioneering his work in the 1930s, Selye was one of the first to recognize people's inherent differences in temperament. He noted that there are "turtles" and "racehorses," and you will never be able to change one into another. Racehorses are born to run. This is demonstrated quite literally in the following spontaneous narrative from another of our workshop participants. She relates the special bond she has created by helping racehorses run well and enabling their owners and trainers to produce winners. (*The "..." below represent significant, meaningful pauses in her delivery, not edits.*)

"I'll never forget the day I saw her in the field... She was this beautiful sorrel filly in the pasture with two other horses...who could never get to me because she was being bullied so badly ... I don't know what it was, maybe because I had been bullied so badly as a child myself, but I connected with this horse... I never dreamt this connection would lead to the first leg of the Triple Crown.

When "Flight" came to the racing barn she acted like a little horse: her head was always down; she was very scared; and yet she was the biggest of the fillies we had. She was wonderfully bred.

That day I decided to dream about the first leg of the Triple Crown. No one believed that she would ever make it, but I did. And I believed in her absolutely. I worked on her for free. I came to her every week and I said, 'Look how big your butt is, just take your head and look around to see how big you are! Lift that head up!' Week after week after week, I worked so that my belief in her became her belief in her.

The night of the trials came and no one believed that Flight could qualify against over 120 horses in fourteen trials. But Flight qualified. None of the other fillies did. Then, no one else believed she could come back and make it into the top in this million-dollar race. She came in second, only beaten by the male horse that would later become World Champion..........

I don't overlook the wallflowers and don't you overlook the wallflowers, especially if the wallflower is you...Take a chance to see what absolute belief will do: it will take you places you never thought you would go...well beyond your comfort zone...and it might just result in something magical that you'll never forget. And lastly, often when we heal others...we find that all along we've just been healing... ourselves."

One of the processes we use in coaching our workshop participants is to have each person stand up and ask for feedback from the group, specifically for the attendees to call out things they liked about her talk, and things that could be improved upon. Here is how the feedback turned out.

The speaker got high praise for the following:

End in mind. This story has a clear message. "Never count yourself out of the running." It is the classic underdog story. It is Rocky Balboa. It is the Little Engine that Could. It is Simba in Disney's The Lion King.

Evoke emotions. There is a powerful reveal in this story that generates empathy and caring. The speaker reveals that, as a young child, she was bullied. Our hearts go out to her. Every parent in the room leaned in when she said those words. The speaker's delivery was really aided by well-timed pauses (...) that allowed the emotional content to register in the minds and hearts of listeners.

Generate tension. Whenever there is a race or any type of contest, what do we want to find out? Who won? This alone keeps us tuned in to see how the story is going to end. We all went along for the ride.

Come full circle. There's a wonderful long pause right before she brings it home and puts forth the key personal message of the story, one that is both universal and other-directed.

Many of our students come into our course as good, even great presenters, but they all want those few nuggets that can take them to the next level. Here were the two minor things that could have improved her story.

The use of unfamiliar terms. You can never assume that your audience is familiar with the jargon and abbreviations in your industry. In this case, most of the audience had no idea that "sorrel" refers to the color of the horse, the reddish-tan to red color of a new penny. Some were unaware that a filly is a young female horse.

Watch out for abbreviations and acronyms. If you are going to use them, make certain to define them right up front in your story. This is of particular importance for the medical profession, whose use of terms can be easily misinterpreted by the general public. A healthcare professional uses the word "chronic" to mean "persistent or long-term;" however, many patients will understand the term to mean "severe." In cancer therapy, the word "positive" can be easily misconstrued, as well. The physician describes "positive" lymph nodes to mean those that show up as positive on a scan, and are cancerous, while the patient interprets "positive" as being "good." According to the National Assessment of Adult Literacy, only 12 percent of US adults have proficient health literacy, a fact that is often easy to overlook.[55]

Abbreviations are also potential sources of confusion. Take the word "oar." There is the oar that is used to propel a boat. But abbreviations using these letters could mean Organ at Risk (for hospitals), Off-Axis Ratio (for radiologists), Office of AIDS (for Public Health Officials), or O.A.R (for millennials, the popular

American rock band). While we have obviously taken the abbreviation out of context, the point is that if you lose people early on in your story with an abbreviation or term they don't understand, you lose them for the entirety of your story. So, be careful in your word selection.

Use all the senses. We can all imagine the filly's "big butt." However, the imagery in this story could have been richer. Without adding too much length to the narrative, there were opportunities to slip in some additional descriptors to really engage all the listener's senses. The speaker could describe the sights and sounds of the racetrack and the excitement of the race itself: the potpourri of smells coming from nervous horses and nervous jockeys; the breezes causing the slight swaying of the horses' tails; the look in Flight's eyes as she entered the track; the palpitations the speaker felt as the filly rounded the bend for home. You get the idea.

Your Place of Power

Just as you have a position of power, you also have your place of power. It's an easy place to locate. Take a moment to answer these questions:

- Where do you feel most at home, comfortable, vibrant, secure and alive?
- What place speaks to your soul?
- Where are you when you feel totally alive, vital and energized?

Close your eyes, take a few deep breaths and visualize the place that comes most vividly to mind.

Once you've got this image, use your senses to paint a compelling, engaging picture of this special location. Mark demonstrates with his story.

157

"The smell does it every time and rightfully it should. The olfactory nerve is our most primitive. It has a direct connection to the brain. For me, it's the smell of jasmine that sets off a cascade of images, sparking my answer to the query, 'Tell me a place where you felt totally alive, vital, and energized.'

My love affair with Portland, Oregon began on a spring day in 1974, when I took my first run on the Wildwood trail high above the Rose Gardens and Arboretum. My feet gently caressed the yielding earth leaving nary a smudge in the patina of pine and fir needles. Green sword ferns stood at attention as I passed them by. Above me stood a canapé of tall evergreens, reaching to touch the puffy white clouds. A gentle mist bathed my face as I pressed forward, my loping stride and breath synchronized to the calming sounds of the forest.

When I turned the corner it hit me. A smell so sweet and so tangy that its memory is burned into my brain. The scent of jasmine. No matter where I am in the world, this fragrance brings me back to Oregon, to the Wildwood trail, to being young and fit, vital, and energized. It is my place of power."

There's a purpose to describing your place of power.

This exercise provides the antidote for an inherent reluctance to release your innate descriptive powers.

So, in honing your story, spend that extra bit of time and attention to use a rich array of descriptors that tingle all the senses and imprint powerful images in your attendees.

Are you thinking: "I'm not good on camera?

Video is one of the best ways to tell your story.

But many of our students feel "I'm not good on camera." It's not because they're "not talented" or "not attractive." It's mostly because they don't know the first thing about how to do a decent looking video. That's because nobody ever showed them what to do.

We would like to change that for you right now.

Download our free *Video Presence Accelerator* training program.

In this free course, we take you step-by-step through the process of designing an entire series of short videos that you can use on your website, Facebook page, and YouTube channel. We show you how to present yourself and your business in a way that attracts exactly the clients, customers or patients you most want to work with. Here's where you can get this free resource right now:

bit.do/changewell

Chapter 8

Help Others Get What They Need

"You give before you get." —Napoleon Hill

"You can have everything in life you want,
if you will just help enough other people get what they want."
—Zig Ziglar

"You're gonna have to serve somebody, yes indeed." —Bob Dylan

So many people have said it in many different ways. The one reliable way to get what we want is to help others get what they need. If we accept that as an obvious, although sometimes inconvenient truth, the next question to ask is: who are we serving and what do they need?

Jordan Belfort is the convicted criminal also known as "the Wolf of Wall Street." His story involves trying to get what you want by cheating others. Having been arrested, convicted, sentenced, and punished, he now turns his experience into value by teaching his own unique (and now ethical) sales method.

His notoriety aside, Belfort is the author of one of our favorite quotes: "The purpose of business is to monetize value." We like it because it invites us to consider value as an asset, and business as a system that transforms wants and desires into an asset that can then, in turn, be transformed into revenues and profits. It does this by creating customers. Customers are people who give us money in exchange for goods and services that make their lives better. We get what we want by giving them what they need.

Here's how we answered the questions "Who are we serving?" and "What do they need?"

We started ChangeWell Training Academy with a theory that later proved to be incorrect. We originally called ourselves "Key Opinion Leader Training Academy," believing that our body of knowledge would strongly appeal to a narrow slice of doctors who wanted to earn fees by speaking persuasively about medical, aesthetic, nutraceutical, and pharmaceutical products. Typically hired by industry, these clinicians and researchers are known as Key Opinion Leaders (KOL). We believed every healthcare professional should strive to be a KOL.

After the better part of a year, we realized our audience was razor thin, and our customer, rather than being the healthcare professional, was really the company whose product needed promoting. This was not the business we wanted to build. We wanted our services to be of value to a much larger audience, including healthcare professionals who were beginning to burn out, but could sense that there might be a better way to identify and attract patients they would like to treat. These professionals required not just the confidence and courage to change, but also the skills and support to create a better future for themselves.

We created a customer avatar—a fictional composite person who embodied the characteristics of physicians whom we thought would be our best customers. This would help us design our business building strategy.

We envisioned that she would most likely be a 40-something female practicing in a metropolitan area in Southern California. She would be well-educated and capable. But she would also be frustrated by the structural changes in healthcare as well as by the astonishing increase in competition and decreased reimbursement, resulting in a big squeeze on her time as well as on the operating margins of her business. We knew she wanted to generate more cash to augment or replace her insurance-based revenue. We theorized that she would like to read books, see movies, and travel in her spare time. We gave her a name, "Jennifer" and then searched Google images for "Dr. Jennifer Pasadena." Up came pictures of several female doctors, all named Jennifer, practicing in cities in and around Pasadena. We picked one and she became the face of our customer avatar.

Dr. Jennifer's profile was never intended to capture every single fact about our customers, nor was she ever meant to be a statistically accurate composite. The purpose of the avatar was to give us the face of a customer. When we created products or content, we always looked at her face and her profile so we could aim our efforts at just one person—a stand-in for our entire customer base.

In our first *EYP* training, most of the participants were female healthcare professionals who closely resembled our avatar. But what we learned from them shocked us.

They told us our training was extraordinarily valuable. But they also told us we had missed the mark by guessing too small.

They told us that our work could apply to anyone, not just in healthcare, but anyone who served people through a profession.

We tested that idea in subsequent weeks and concluded that our customers were right. We needed to re-name, re-brand, and re-focus on a larger audience.

Working with our clients, we always suggest that they create a customer avatar to put a human face on their efforts to market and promote their business. In fact, it could be useful to segment your target market and have a different avatar for every product line. The single biggest reason is so that you have a starting point to create your presence and then focus it at the target customer.

Next, we tackle the question: once you have identified your customer, what do they need? There are a couple of ways to go at this. You could do it directly by observing who buys what you sell. After an ample number of transactions, you will begin to notice a pattern that represents the core of your business. It's important to identify the core because the Pareto Principle, or 80/20 Rule, tells us that you will make 80% of your revenue from just 20% of your total customer base. It's very important to know who those 20% are.

We know a couple of auto dealers who require each customer to fill out a survey before they get the keys to their new car. The survey provides data that doesn't seem significant, but when aggregated, it's very powerful. Imagine knowing the age, zip codes, gender, and media usage habits of each person who bought Toyota Corollas from your dealership. If you knew that, you could precisely target your advertising. You could compare your sales to Department of Motor Vehicle registrations by make and model and see if there were other geographies that you could tap into.

By aggregating the data, you would not only have statistics, but you could also get to know customers who represent the largest slice of buyers. You could employ that information to create ads with faces and voices that sound like your customers. Advertising created like this conveys a strong sense of presence: "Seems like they are talking to me!" They are.

Another way to zero in your core customers is to use the metrics associated with your website and social media pages. When you look at the demographics of your Facebook page, you will find information about the gender, age range, and geography of the people who follow you. You can see which of your posts they like and share with others. This data can help you begin to answer the question: "who is my best customer and what do they need from me?"

Having a clearly defined picture of your ideal customer is important because the relevance of the message is the difference between "junk mail" and "valuable information". When you get the right message, to the right person, in the right manner, at the right time, good things are more likely to happen. Certainly you could make some money. Beyond that, you will also have the experience of genuinely helping people who need and want what you have.

If you don't have customers yet, you can start as we did—with a good guess—and update as you gather customers and experience.

It's important at this point to distinguish between "want" and "need."

Put Your Customers on the Ladder

Abraham Harold Maslow was an American psychologist who was best known for creating Maslow's Hierarchy of Needs. This is a theory of psychological health based upon a prioritization of human needs ranging from subsistence at the base to self-actualization at the apex. Maslow believed that people can work their way up the pyramid; however, very few people make it to the top.

MASLOW'S HIERACHY OF NEEDS

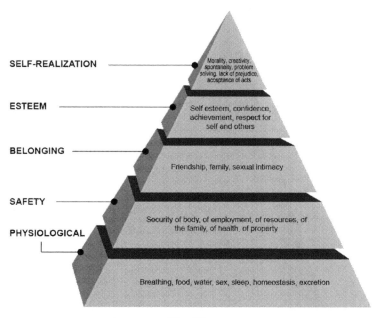

SELF-REALIZATION — Morality, creativity, spontaneity, problem solving, lack of prejudice, acceptance of acts

ESTEEM — Self esteem, confidence, achievement, respect for self and others

BELONGING — Friendship, family, sexual intimacy

SAFETY —

PHYSIOLOGICAL — Security of body, of employment, of resources, of the family, of health, of property

Breathing, food, water, sex, sleep, homeostasis, excretion

Fig. 12

Maslow's hierarchy (Fig. 12) says that when more basic needs go unmet, this prevents us from stretching higher. You may want a Tesla (Esteem), but you need to pay the rent this month (Safety). Assuming logical behavior, no matter how much you might *want* a luxury electric car, if the choice is Tesla or eviction, you will find a way to pay the rent because you *need* to.

Look at your customer avatar, then locate that person on the Maslow hierarchy. This will give you some provocative insights into product creation and messaging.

To show you how this would work, let's assume that you are doing well selling real estate as an independent agent. You have an electronic database with the names, emails, and phone numbers of the many young families to whom you have sold homes. Your personal website is up and functioning to promote your brokerage abilities. If you wanted to add some incremental revenue, you might begin by offering some safety-related products and services. You could consider ads from one of the credit monitoring or identity theft companies. You could consider various home tech devices like security systems, cameras, remotely operated thermostats. How about services like property & casualty insurance, investment advisories, and financial planning?

While you have no hard proof that your existing customers are in the market for those items, by looking at Maslow's hierarchy, you could develop some pretty strong hunches that you could then test. (Of course, there are other, more sophisticated, market segment analyses you could do.) But the point here is that you can use commonly available psychological knowledge to identify customer needs that create business opportunities.

The ChangeWell Customer

At ChangeWell, our typical customer has satisfied their basic physiological needs. They have handled the basics such as food clothing and shelter. But that doesn't mean they are all in the same situation. For some, their job situation is challenging for reasons including changes in their profession, shifts in government regulations, or significant increases in competition.

Some of our customers have been in their chosen profession long enough to know that they don't want to do that any more. But they don't know what comes next. They may feel like they want to branch out, start over, or totally switch professions. They may need business planning, financial counseling, graduate education, or legal advice. ChangeWell doesn't do any of that.

If there is a single driving force in the life of ChangeWell's ideal customer, it's the need for professional esteem, respect, and success. We aim all of our products and services right at this need. Our messaging centers on that need.

We do our best to deliver real and tangible value that makes a difference. We raise the bar by pointing towards outcomes that lead our clients to become self-actualized contributors to society. As we see it, that's what they need. That's why this book is subtitled *The Path to Personal Power, Professional Influence, and Business Results.* We hope it's catchy and memorable. We intend for it to reach and motivate the customer we most want to serve. For us, the highest reward is when a client tells us we've helped them move ahead to achieve what they want.

What Else do Others Need from Us?

It's true. People who attend your presentation are there to be informed.

Do you think that there's a shortage of available information out there? Maybe in the pre-Google days when we were children and our content choices were *Encyclopedia Britannica* and *World Book.*

Then why are so many presenters guilty of trying to get participants to take a drink from their facts-and-figures-laden firehose?

Sure, people do need information; they need the facts. But what most people *really need* from most presenters (even the most academic ones) is to be *moved* and *inspired*. At some level—often subliminal—they want you to strike an emotional chord in them.

Presenters and persuaders often make the erroneous assumption that people make their buying decisions on logic alone. But the emerging science of behavioral economics, a blend of psychology and financial decision-making analysis, paints a different story. While we may initially focus on the numbers when making buying decisions (e.g. for a car, how many miles to the gallon, the cost of maintenance, the size of the trunk), in many cases the decision and the purchase is based upon subliminal emotional elements. (I love the way it makes me feel; it's a great color; the lights are so cool.) It's now believed that most decision-making is done at the non-conscious or emotional level.

Dale Carnegie's classic book, *How to Win Friends and Influence People,* perhaps said it best:

> *"When dealing with people, let us remember we are not dealing with creatures of logic. We are dealing with creatures of emotion, creatures bristling with prejudices and motivated by pride and vanity."*

Coming from the Heart

As our *EYP* seminar gains renown, we are increasingly drawing high-logic individuals such as engineers, financial planners, architects, lawyers, scientists, surgeons and dentists into the course. Many of these professionals recognize that something seems to be missing in their approach to selling, presenting, or influencing.

Somewhere along the line they have received feedback that they should:

"Speak from the heart."

"Make your remarks more heartfelt."

Or that their approach needs "more emotion," "greater warmth," or "stronger connections" with others.

The heart is often regarded as the center of emotion. And for these more highly logical types, it often plays a distant second fiddle to the brain. High-logic individuals subscribe to the seventeenth-century French philosopher René Descartes' famous formulation, "Cogito ergo sum:" I think, therefore I am. Highly analytical people are often oblivious to the river of emotion that runs through life, connecting people via the tributaries of empathy and caring. Hence the rising popularity of business courses that teach emotional intelligence.

The Neurophysiology of Emotion

There is a growing body of research to support the primacy of the heart in the communication process. Maybe the ancient Egyptians weren't all wrong when they believed that the heart, rather than the brain was the center of life and morality. Consider that:

The heart sends more signals to the brain than the brain sends to the heart.

The heart communicates to the brain in four different ways.

- **The nervous system**: Your brain and heart are wired together by the nervous system. Neural pathways connect the heart to the amygdala, the portion of the brain that is directly involved in processing emotion. When there is a disturbance in the heart's rhythm, signals are sent to the brain. The brain translates this information into emotions such as anxiety, or unease.

- **Hormone biochemistry:** The heart is also communicating to the brain biochemically, via the release of hormones and neurotransmitters, chemical secreted into the blood stream. The heart was reclassified as an endocrine gland (like adrenals, ovaries, testicles) in 1983 when it was found that both the upper chamber and lower heart chambers secreted peptides that influence blood pressure and blood volume. These same peptides have also been found in the brain nerve cells.

- **Biophysical communication**. The heart generates pulse waves as it goes through the mechanical phases of contraction and relaxation. These pulse waves are felt by the brain as well as by other organs.

- **Electromagnetic Fields.** From a communication and presentation standpoint, this is perhaps the most exciting form of cardiac communication. Simply put: your heart emits an electromagnetic field. As we describe below, this magnetic field not only influences *your* brain, it also connects to the hearts and brains of others around you, influencing *theirs*.

The field of cardioelectric communication and the role that heart rate variability plays in human health and performance has been extensively studied by HeartMath Institute (heartmath.org), an organization that conducts research and works with educators, non-profits and first responders in learning coherence techniques (see below). In their monograph *Science of the Heart Volume 2*, the authors state:

> The heart is the most powerful source of electromagnetic energy in the human body, producing the largest rhythmic electromagnetic field of any of the body's organs. The heart's electrical field is about 60 times greater in amplitude than the electrical activity generated by the brain. This field, measured in the form of an electrocardiogram (ECG) can be detected anywhere on the surface of the body. Furthermore, the magnetic field produced by the heart is more than 100 times greater in strength than the field generated by the brain and can be detected up to 3 feet away from the body, in all directions, using SQUID based magnetometers.[56]

In the course of our *EYP* trainings, we will often connect soon-to-be presenting and somewhat anxious attendees to the HeartMath Inner Balance™ Trainer and app (readily available online). This system provides simple visual biofeedback using colors. In just a few minutes we help our student achieve "coherence," which is a balanced state of breathing, coupled with feelings of gratitude, that together exert a calming effect on the nervous system.

We do this by teaching the Quick Coherence® Technique-to our attendees:

- Step 1: Heart-Focused Breathing. Focus your attention in the area of the heart. Imagine your breath is flowing in and out of your heart or chest area, breathing a little slower and deeper than usual.
- Step 2: Activate a Positive Feeling. Make a sincere attempt to experience a regenerative feeling such as appreciation or care for someone or something in your life.

- Suggestion: Inhale 5 seconds, exhale 5 seconds (or whatever rhythm is comfortable). Putting your attention around the heart area helps you center and get coherent.

- Suggestion: Try to re-experience the feeling you have for someone you love, a pet, a special place, and accomplishment etc., or focus on a feeling of calm or ease.[57]

The first advantage of the Quick Coherence Technique is obvious. It calms the jitters of a nervous presenter. But it's the second advantage that takes the technique into the realm of giving others what they need; namely, a heart-felt connection to you and your message. By you focusing on positive feelings, ideally other-centered, you then radiate this energy directly to the hearts and minds of those around you.

Generating Emotional Resonance

Regardless of how much weight you place on brain versus heart, it's clear that there is a set of techniques that you can use to generate emotional resonance with your remarks. Here are a few tips:

Incorporate Emotional Language into Your Speech

If you wish to evoke feelings, try incorporating more feeling-oriented words in your dialogue, such as those noted below.

- Value
- Share
- Trust
- Feel
- Cherish
- Honor
- Admire
- Grieve
- Empathize
- Love
- Believe
- Care for

For maximum impact, pair the words with gestures emanating or connecting to your heart. Soften your tone of voice. The degree to which you use emotional language depends upon the nature of your audience and their receptivity to these terms. Pardon the generalization to follow, but: you could calibrate your remarks based upon whether you are speaking mainly to feeling-oriented people (social workers, school teachers, nurses), or analytics (scientists, engineers, accountants). Even better, sprinkle your presentation with these feeling words and note the type of reaction you are getting from the audience. If you see heads nod, bodies move slightly toward you, and feel hearts connect, feel free to increase your use of emotional language.

Get Your Heart on Camera

YouTube has changed the world. Now that everyone can be a video star, many people feel they have to be. That is—until they actually try appearing on video. It can be disheartening indeed to try so hard to appear to be warm, friendly, kind, helpful and fun, only to discover that you don't look or sound that way at all.

There is no doubt that delivering a script direct to a camera is challenging. It's a skill that can be developed with practice.

Most people come off far better in an interview. What we've found in videotaping on-camera interviews is that the second half of the interview is invariably much better that than first half. The subject of the interview calms down, and gets focused. They find their tone and pacing. A bit more passion comes across.

Here's the problem: your viewers are impatient. They want you to get right to the best stuff quickly. They can't wait until the second half.

Here are two questions that will automatically tap into who you are, and why you do what you do. Give these questions to the person who will be interviewing you. Encourage them to ask these questions at the beginning of the video session:

What led you to choose your current specialty? Most professionals can tap into their passion by reliving the "aha" moment when their purpose and path became clear. This natural enthusiasm is the antidote to the flat, matter-of-fact tone of voice that pervades so many interviews.

The second question is equally simple: **What do you find rewarding about your current work?** Make sure the answer is about you helping people. What happens to you when you see someone's life change because of what you do? Your narrative begins the process of creating an emotional bond with your audience. And that's the most important quality of an effective video.

Slip in Emotionally Impactful Videos

We often use inspiring, short video clips in our presentations. The images, words and music create a shared, and somewhat different atmosphere. The video medium allows for an attention reset; it also has the advantage of being pre-produced and consistent. In a longer program, it's a great time for you to step to the side of the stage, grab a throat drop, a sip of water, and watch for audience reactions. Three of our favorites are:

- *Gratitude* by Louis Schwartzberg. A beautiful global cinematic experience that helps open our eyes and appreciate the beauty around us.
  https://www.youtube.com/watch?v=2egMSliB8DE
- *Never, Ever Give Up. Arthur's Inspirational Transformation!* Tells the story of a disabled former soldier who regains health through the practice of yoga.
  https://www.youtube.com/watch?v=qX9FSZJu448
- *Enjoy Every Sandwich Book Trailer.*
  https://www.youtube.com/watch?v=3UIFbOfWwYET
  The story of the late Lee Lipsenthal, MD, one of the grandfathers of the Integrative Health Movement. Lee describes how esophageal cancer sharpened his focus to deeply connect with others. His book of the same title helps people find joy in the simplicity of every moment. We often invoke Lee's spirit when we put forth his powerful quote about the process of transformation, described in the next chapter.

Pain will push you until vision starts to pull you.
–Dr. Lee Lipsenthal

Chapter 9

Be Open to Transformation

*"You don't make friends with an elephant trainer
unless you have room in your house for an elephant."*
—Sufi Expression

For many years, Mark had a cartoon picture above his desk at work. It showed a person going through an old-fashioned hand clothes wringer. Half of the person appeared normal; the part that had gone through the wringer was pancake-flat. The title of the cartoon provided the punch line. It said, "The truth will set you free, but first it will make you miserable."

He kept this cartoon to help him remember that—for the patients he was working with—making meaningful life changes is not easy. There is always a level of contemplation, and an equal or greater dose of discomfort, involved in change. In fact, in our *EYP* classes, we throw participants into exercises that are intended to take them out of their comfort zones and initially make them somewhat uncomfortable. This process mobilizes their energy and helps them get over inertia. By the end of the day, those who experience the greatest breakthroughs in their performance demonstrate a willingness to not only take risks but also to share their vulnerabilities with others. These participants are more willing to "open the kimono" and grow by disclosing some of their inner thoughts and feelings.

Personal Disclosure: How Much is the Right Amount?

There is a time and place for personal disclosure. One of the most effective uses is in the manager-subordinate relationship. Bosses really only do two things: they direct and they support. Direction is pretty obvious. The boss tells you what, when, where, how—and hopefully why. She checks your work and ideally offers suggestions for correction.

Support is another thing. It can be motivational and inspirational, ranging from "atta boy," "atta girl," and "keep up the great work" to more meaningful assistance. There's instrumental support such as providing needed training, resources or authority. Leaders also support their people when they catch them doing things right and offer timely, actionable feedback and praise.

There's another type of support, however, that can be incredibly effective in building bonds of trust and loyalty: self-disclosure on the leader's part. This type of self-disclosure is done in a quiet time and place, when both giver and recipient are present. It is most impactful when used at a point of subordinate vulnerability, a time when a mistake has been made. It goes something like this:

Boss: You know, Mary, when I had your position I had some of the very same issues and challenges. In fact, one time, I too made a really careless mistake. Let me tell you about it....

The leader's personal disclosure goes a long way to letting the subordinate know that she is not alone; she is neither the first, nor the last, to make mistakes. Revealing some of one's background, frailty and mistakes also humanizes the boss. It creates a culture of loyalty and engenders trust.

It's much less clear how much personal disclosure should take place in the other direction, from subordinate to boss; or, for that matter, between peers. As the modified saying goes, "Familiarity breeds attempt." Disclosing vulnerabilities in competitive environments can lead to this information being used against you.

In a time when all of us are projecting our presence digitally, on websites and in social media outlets, the question of self-disclosure in the professional setting takes on even greater importance.

So where does the balance lie? In the quest for the authenticity that is key to presence, what is appropriate to share? In other words, how far should you open the kimono?

A Construct for Disclosure

In 1955, two psychologists, Joseph Luft and Harrington Ingham, developed a simple grid to help people better understand themselves and how they relate to others. Adopting their first names, they called the grid the Johari Window. Luft and Ingham created an exercise in which the subjects were provided with a list of adjectives and were instructed to select those they felt best described their personality. They then had their peers rate them using the same adjectives. These adjectives were then placed in four quadrants, as shown on the following page. [58]

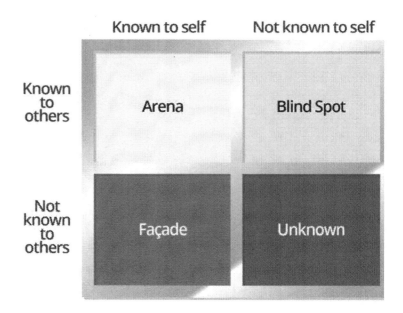

- In the upper left quadrant, often called the Open or Arena quadrant, are the traits that we know about ourselves, and that are readily visible to others.
- The upper right quadrant reveals our Blind Spot. This "room" contains information and traits that others see and know about us, but that we ourselves are unaware of.
- In the lower left quadrant lies the Façade. In this case there is information others do not know about us. We may choose to disclose this information or not. It is a private space.
- The bottom right room represents the unconscious or subconscious part of us that neither others nor we are aware of.

EYP: Guiding Transformation

If one looks at the etymology of the word "transformation," it is not difficult to parse its meaning: trans-formation, with the prefix "trans" meaning "across." To transform is to move across forms, from one to another. Transformation takes place in movement.

Here, in the Johari Window, transformation is the movement from one quadrant to another. For example, this could mean taking traits—both positive and negative—to which we are blind, and moving them to the left of the Window, making them known. Or, transformation could also mean allowing a bit of our Façade to crumble as we share some inner thoughts, feelings and experiences with the group. Let's take a closer look at some of the types of transformation that support presence enhancement.

Playing to Larger Arenas

Today, presence is reflected not just in one-to-one interactions. We also choose how much to reveal in social media. For service providers, particularly in healthcare, this disclosure may serve to attract a certain type of patient or client.

Jill Carnahan, MD, a functional medicine practitioner from Louisville, Colorado makes no secret that she has personally battled both breast cancer and Crohn's disease (jillcarnahan.com). "Dr. Jill" (as she is known to her patients) tells her story front and center on her website, a story that begins with finding an unusual lump in her breast during medical training. The subsequent diagnosis of ductal carcinoma, an aggressive form of breast cancer, was devastating. In the process of beating the cancer, Carnahan went from doctor to patient, from a healthy 25-year-old to a bald (from chemotherapy), malnourished shadow of herself.

Soon after completing therapy and returning to medical school, she was diagnosed with Crohn's disease, a painful and usually chronic autoimmune disease, in which the body's own immune system attacks the gastrointestinal lining. This results in pain, malnutrition, and fever. Told by her gastroenterologist that her only options were medication and surgery, Dr. Jill sought a better way. She turned to the healing power of nutritious food and dietary changes as well as an unwavering faith in God. Today she is symptom-free and radiantly healthy.

Dr. Jill is a highly sought-after speaker. Her authenticity and presence on stage mirror the openness she displays online. It is clear to all who encounter her—either in person or on her website—what she thinks and what she believes in. Hence, she tends to attract complicated patients who have struggled with metabolic, autoimmune, and GI conditions for whom conventional care has failed to provide the answers.

Her coherence in messaging, based on deeply held beliefs, and an equally deep knowledge base, is allowing Dr. Jill to expand her influence. In the language of the Johari window, she is expanding her "Arena," playing to ever-larger audiences because she knows who she is, and those who come in contact with her do as well.

The Blind Spot: John's Story

For the automotive industry the advent of sophisticated lane-changing warning systems has all but eliminated the dangerous blind spot, the disregard of which causes countless accidents. Wouldn't it be great if we could embed the same detector in people so they could be alerted to the blind spots in their demeanor and take corrective action to become more likeable?

John, an older, baby-boomer physician, is a self-described rebel fighting against the conventional healthcare system. Even as a knowledgeable physician, he has been personally harmed by misdiagnosis and complications from procedures. Some people would describe him as cranky, and a bit cantankerous. He initially comes across as an angry crusader, with plenty of blame to lay on large corporations that are contributing to the systematic demise of American's health (e.g. environmental toxins, ever-present fructose, unnecessary antibiotics in feed, genetically modified organisms, etc.). John has spent the last decade immersing himself in the emerging science of Functional and Anti-aging medicine.

When asked what he wanted from the *EYP* session, he said he wanted to build his personal functional medicine practice. As a diligent student of the literature, a devoted conference attendee, and a fellow in the appropriate societies, he had a lot to offer his prospective patients.

The problem was the disconnect between how he regarded himself, and what, in the course of the exercises and feedback from the group, was revealed to be his blind spot: the angry demeanor that others sometimes perceived in him.

After John conducted one particular exercise and requested feedback from the group, one of the members paused for what seemed like an eternity, looked at John, and delivered this feedback:

"John, you have an amazing smile. It's a beautiful smile, and combined with your eyes and a softer tone to your voice, you look like a doctor I want to go see. I think you should smile more."

The measuring stick of personal growth and ultimately successful change is in large measure how well one takes personal feedback. And then, assuming the feedback is true and actionable, what one does with it.

What happened as a result of this feedback? John broke out in a huge smile, an affirmation that he had heard, loud and clear, what was lovingly said to him. Some weeks later, he showed us a video he had just done—one in which he was no longer the angry doctor, but a warm and smiling "magnet" to draw patients to come see him.

This is not to say that fixing blind spots is easy. People cling to them for want of anything better. They may be a big part of one's identity. And the reveal is often accompanied by great personal discomfort. Ideally people can find something of beauty in themselves and a better sense of how they come across to others. In this case John was blind to his own "likeability factor."

There is one universal blind spot that we often call to attention, a positive learning for which we have research to support our observation. According to one psychology study, presenters are often blind to the fact that they come across better than they think they do. The experiment found that speakers consistently rate themselves as more nervous than the audience perceives them to be. In this and other studies, researchers have found that merely informing speakers that their nervousness is not visible often makes them feel less nervous.[59] Consider yourself informed.

The Crumbling of the Façade: Karen's Story

In our *EYP* trainings, we witness incredible moments of soul-bearing, and of acceptance. We have seen participants

184

experience moments of catharsis they did not expect to have. We have heard "wounded healers" speak about their trauma. We've heard stories of great personal loss, even tales of abuse and violence. We have listened to publicity-shy people explore the cause of their insecurities. It is a humbling, touching experience when these participants are received with affirmation and encouragement by the group. We do not need to facilitate this response from the other participants: it is a natural human instinct, an empathic recognition of our shared humanity.

These moments of soul-bearing are a testament to the nature of presence. Presence cannot be just a professional quality. It requires an authenticity, a display of one's true personality, which no skin-deep projection can match. In this book, we have already discussed the common perception—and the fear—that superior presentation skills require a "slick" persona or a professional superficiality. Indeed, sometimes a professional façade is a mask for deep insecurities.

From the moment Karen entered the room, she commanded the attention of both the men and women. Tall, statuesque and professional, she radiated confidence. She clearly had her display together: she was the best-dressed attendee in the class. In her one-on-one sales work, Karen said she exuded confidence, and it was easy for all to believe her.

When it came time for her to tell a "story of significance" to the group, she broke down into a cascade of tears, accompanied by violent shaking. She told the story of having to give a big presentation to her new management team. And she blew it. She froze. She was hesitant. She rambled on. The presentation was, according to her, "a disaster." It took a good ten minutes until she was able to regain her composure.

The attendees were shocked. Somehow, they had difficulty resolving this new image with Karen's previous calm, cool and collected outer appearance. But we all know that we learn many times more from our failures than from our successes. If we are willing to honestly address and learn from these moments, "failures" become our greatest source of strength. With the support of the group, Karen was able to recast this moment as a valuable life lesson. She attacked the remainder of the class with attentiveness and vigor, and probably came further in her abilities than any of the other attendees that day.

The last quadrant of the Window—unknown to us and unknown to others—takes us into unknown territory. In the course of presenting and persuading others—from the standpoint of belief and authenticity, "stuff" comes up for people, some of it seemingly from left field. Images come to mind, many from childhood; stories long buried in the subconscious; the echoed words of loved ones. And we wonder where this comes from.

Going with the Flow

It makes perfect sense that people routinely rediscover long-hidden memories, feelings, and abilities when they are tapping into their genuine selves for the first time (or the fiftieth). Because when a speaker opens herself up to her audience, it is truly a transformative, even transcendent experience—for both her listeners and for her. We often see this at our workshops. Participants who speak to the group with vulnerability, authenticity, and presence are experiencing the moment on another level, and it shows visibly in their performance. Such speakers are in the "flow."

You may have heard of this concept. First theorized by Hungarian psychologist Mihaly Csikszentmihalyi, the "flow state" is "the holistic experience that people feel when they act with total involvement." [60] Csikszentmihalyi developed the concept of "flow" by observing artists while they worked. He found that they were often more motivated by their enjoyment of the *process* of creating than by any external gains (such as financial success, improved social status, or getting to keep the art objects they produced). This creative process was almost mystical: artists would often enter into the "flow" of complete immersion while painting.[61]

Csikszentmihalyi later sought to confirm this hunch about flow through his now-famous Beeper Studies. He would give groups of participants pagers that would ping at random times during the day. The participants would then record the emotions and thoughts they were experiencing whenever the pager went off. Although the feelings that people recorded were mostly unhappy, Csikszentmihalyi discovered that they tended to experience more positive emotions when engaged in a fairly challenging activity—one that's not too easy, and not too hard. This mid-level difficulty is the sweet spot that activities must hit in order to induce flow.[62]

During flow, Csikszentmihalyi observed, we experience "A sense that [our] skills are adequate to cope with the challenges at hand ... Self-consciousness disappears, and the sense of time becomes distorted."[63] Clearly, these are all desirable states to be in while one is giving a presentation. But getting into the flow won't just help you calm down. It will also help you connect with your audience. When you, the presenter, are in flow, your audience is also more likely to feel that flow along with you.

They lose track of the time, and focus on a single task: listening to you.

Time to Get to Work

How can we get to a high enough level of comfort with an activity—like public speaking—that we can "flow" while doing it? Chances are you've heard about the 10,000-hour rule that Malcolm Gladwell describes in his book, *Outliers.* Gladwell was referring to the important role of *deliberate* practice in developing mastery. He referenced a study of musicians conducted by Anders Ericsson in the early 1990s.

Ericsson compared elite professional violinists from world-class symphony orchestras with three groups of student violinists at a prestigious music school. Professors identified the students they believed would go on to have careers as international soloists. They also identified those students whom they believed would become good violinists, and those who would most likely end up as music teachers. Through diaries and interviews with the musicians, Ericsson showed how practice paid off. The best violinists accumulated more than 10,000 hours of practice, compared with 8,000 for the good group, and 4,000 hours for the music teachers. In his study, he noted that the best violinists practiced close to their maximum. Studies of other groups, like writers and pianists, showed similar results. It certainly makes sense that, the more you practice, the better you get.

However, a recent analysis of 88 studies by researchers at Princeton[64] has cast doubt on this long-held assertion of the primacy of time spent practicing to develop mastery. The researchers found that practice accounted for only a 12% difference in performance across a host of domains. There was a wide discrepancy, depending upon the activity being studied. For example:

- In games, practice accounted for a 26% difference
- In music, it was a 21% difference
- In sports, an 18% difference
- In education, a 4% difference
- In professions, only a 1% difference

The study's lead author, Brooke Macnamara, noted that, "There is no doubt that deliberate practice is important, from both a statistical and a theoretical perspective. It is just less important than has been argued."

What's the take-home message for readers of this book who want to improve their presence skills? The answer lies not just in the *quantity* of time spent learning and mastering new skills, but also in the *quality* of the practice. And quality can be augmented.

For example, if you want to become a better jazz piano player, a coach can help you understand what jazz is all about. He can teach you the musical scales, and help you put chords together on the fly. Then the deliberate practice will take you to the next level. On the other hand, you can deliberately practice "Twinkle, Twinkle, Little Star" by yourself multiple times a day, but you'll never learn the improvisational skills that comprise jazz.

What we have seen be maximally effective is directed practice of specific skills in the presence of a coach.

The Outcomes of Coaching

Of course, the more professional the coaching, the more effective the practice. We have written this book with the goal of providing you with a portable mini-coach, with lessons on specific skills in every page. For these lessons, we've drawn on our in-person coaching, conducted during the *EYP* workshops. We know that this coaching is effective because we have seen it work.

Through their own victories, workshop participants have validated the seven principles of presence and, in the process, taught us how to be more effective coaches. We have been honored to:

- Observe the setting of intentions and the direction of undistracted, undivided attention towards others.
- See people re-order to put "being" ahead of "doing" and "having."
- Hear stories of love, loss and every emotion in between, told with conviction and passion.
- Witness quantum leaps in presentation abilities: hooking us with the open, informing us with gestures, moving in sync with words, and sticking the landing.
- Observe the breakdown of barriers to genuine interpersonal communication as presenters take risks by revealing their authentic personalities, candidly sharing their fears and hopes with their audience.
- Give and receive feedback in a loving, non-biased, supportive environment.
- See attendees crystallize their unique message and deliver this both in-person and on video.

Perhaps most impactful have been the moments when presenters reveal a passion and a drive that derives from other-centeredness. These presentations that ignite a possibility for others, that imagine a shared future, are often the most touching and inspiring.

Honor the Power of Your Influence

We usually begin our workshops with what we call an influence audit. Very simply, we ask the assembled two-dozen participants how many people's lives they may touch in the course of a year. The numbers range, from physicians who have 3,000 patients, to accountants with dozens of clients, to caregivers whose work revolves around a few people. We routinely total the number, then multiply this number by 2.5, to account for friends and families. It is not uncommon for this number to easily equal or exceed 100,000 lives.

This is the potential power of presence: not Mark and Robert's, but the collective presence of those in the room. This is why we believe so strongly in our work. Every day, with every *EYP* training course we lead or with every copy of this book that we put into the hands of others, we keep this figure in mind: 100,000 lives or more. That is how many people are potentially affected by the presence of even a small group. It is simply our exercise in "crunching the numbers" that has led us to believe that the work of enhancing presence is work with the potential to change the world. For the two of us, the chance to do this work is the highest privilege imaginable.

We encourage you to honor the power of your influence. You should enhance your presence because you have a presence that is worth enhancing. You have the potential to be a positive influence on the lives of so many others. You have a message that is worthwhile for other people to hear. If the lessons of our book can help you deliver that message with increased clarity and conviction, then we are humbled to have been of service.

Take the Next Step

You can only learn so much from reading and viewing. If you are ready to take your presentation, persuasion, and promotion skills to the next level, consider attending one of our one- or two-day live *EYP* Training programs. We'll provide you with small group and individual coaching to help you:

- Attract, engage, retain and grow your best customers
- Sharpen your message; increase its appeal and persuasive power
- Present your ideas confidently & effectively before a group of any size
- Enhance the impact of your voice, posture, gestures, and movement
- Overcome any anxiety that gets in your way
- "Sell" your products, services, and ideas with confidence
- Use the power of video to extend your professional influence
- Project an engaging, compelling social media presence
- Immediately apply what you have learned to your life and work

If you are seeking a breakthrough in presenting your ideas, this course will jump start your proficiency and confidence. If you are already an accomplished presenter, this course will fortify your presentation with new skills that you can use immediately. You will find our quarterly schedule of trainings at www.changewell.com or write to us at:

info@changewell.com

Theory vs Practice

We are very big on teaching "how things work." But we know that nothing happens by theory alone.

So we are offering some practical guidance on how to put the ideas in this book to work for you in a way that enhances your presence.

Download our free *Video Presence Accelerator* training course.

We guide you through the process of creating a series of short videos that use features and benefits in a way that attracts the clients, customers, & patients you really want. This free training covers:

• How to design and present your message.

• How to use equipment you already have to actually create your videos. All you need is your cell phone and our pro level production tips.

You'll also receive a detailed e-book that reveals the techniques we use to create our popular video blog series. You get both. To get your free course, go to:

bit.do/changewell

Want to Stay in Touch with Us?

Follow us on:

Facebook

- www.facebook.com/changewellinc

LinkedIn

- Mark: www.linkedin.com/in/marktager
- Robert: www.linkedin.com/in/therobertjohnhughes

Twitter

- Mark: @marktager
- Robert: @robertjhnhughes

About the Authors

Mark J. Tager, MD.

Dr. Mark Tager is CEO of ChangeWell Inc., a San Diego based company that guides organizations and individuals to higher levels of performance. Along with Robert John Hughes, he is co-founder of Changewell Training Academy, which enables professionals to amplify their influence.

A veteran of more than 800 presentations, Mark shares his skills and passion to empower those who attend his trainings. He brings a rich background to his work in leadership, organizational development and personal wellbeing. As an entrepreneur, he has built successful businesses and managed high performance teams. As a consultant and change agent, he has worked with a broad spectrum of organizations, from Fortune 100 companies to small non-profits. As a physician, he is well grounded in aesthetic, lifestyle, regenerative and integrative medicine.

Mark founded Great Performance, Inc., a healthcare publishing and training company that was acquired by Times Mirror and integrated into Mosby medical publishing. He has served as Director of Health Promotion for Kaiser Permanente in Oregon, as the founding marketing VP for the Fraxel™ laser, and as Chief Marketing Officer for Syneron. A highly sought after speaker, Mark lectures internationally for a number of medical device, nutraceutical, cosmeceutical and biotech companies. He currently provides consulting for health-related companies that want to crystallize their professional and consumer messaging.

He has authored nine books related to health and performance including *Total Engagement: The Healthcare Practitioner's Guide to Heal Yourself, Your Patients and Your Practice* (With Mimi Guarneri, MD), *The Art of Aesthetic Practice* (with Stephen Mulholland, MD), *Leadership in Times of Stress and Change*, and *Transforming Stress into Power*. Mark attended Duke University Medical School and trained in family practice at The Oregon Health & Science University.

Robert John Hughes

Robert John Hughes is a marketing strategist, brand advocate and media business entrepreneur. His expertise includes the fields of marketing, advertising, business consulting, leadership training, public relations, journalism, and broadcasting. He is co-founder of ChangeWell Training Academy.

Robert is a former White House news correspondent for a major American broadcaster. During his career he interviewed some of the most notable figures in American politics and government. He is the author of *How to Write a One Page News Release – Make Your Own News and Get it Covered for Free.*

Following the journalism phase of his career, Robert entered radio station management first as an award winning news director at WASH-FM, Washington, DC. He became the station's Program Director and developed the Adult Contemporary music format, which has become one of the most listened to forms of radio in America today. He was appointed station manager at

WXTR in Washington, DC where he more than doubled the station's value in three years. Robert was a co-founder and President of US Radio which became one of the four largest American radio companies. In the early 90s, bucking the Wall Street financed consolidation of the radio business, he led the formation of Compass Radio Group, that owned six locally managed stations in St Louis, Phoenix, and San Diego.

Turning his writing and producing skills to the field of advertising, he has created marketing campaigns for thousands of clients. His copywriting, directing, and producing talents have won him the coveted Mercury Award as well as several ADDY Awards from the American Advertising Federation.

His management consulting clients include Aetna Insurance, Heller Financial, and Chrysler Capital. As a voice over narrator, he has performed for a host of international brands including Starbucks, Porsche, Ingersoll-Rand, La Prairie, Lockheed Martin, United Bank of Switzerland, Volkswagen/Audi, Harman Kardon, Samsung, China Tourism, and Macy's.

Throughout his career, Robert has lectured and taught subjects as diverse as media and politics, advertising and marketing, and self-expression and leadership. He graduated from Fordham University in New York with a degree in English and Mass Media.

Index

Notes

[1] Weber Shandwick, "Millennials@Work: Perspectives on Reputation," 2015, https://www.webershandwick.com/news/article/millennials-at-work-perspectives-on-reputation.

[2] Plato, *Plato's Phaedrus*, trans. Reginald Hackforth (Cambridge, England: Cambridge University Press, 1952).

[3] Pam Mueller and Daniel Oppenheimer, "The Pen is Mightier than the Keyboard: Advantages of Longhand over Laptop Note Taking," *Psychological Science* 25, no. 6 (January 16, 2014): 1159–1168.

[4] Donovan Livingston, "Lift Off," May 25, 2016, http://www.gse.harvard.edu/news/16/05/lift.

[5] Dominique Autier-Dérian et al., "Visual Discrimination of Species in Dogs (Canis Familiaris)," *Animal Cognition* 16, no. 4 (July 2013): 637-51.

[6] Microsoft Canada, "Attention Spans," Spring 2015, https://advertising.microsoft.com/en/WWDocs/User/display/cl/researchreport/31966/en/microsoft-attention-spans-research-report.pdf.

[7] *Oxford Dictionaries, s.v.* "charisma," accessed June 14, 2013, http://www.oxforddictionaries.com/us/definition/american_english/charisma.

[8] Max Weber, *Economy and Society: An Outline of Interpretive Sociology*, ed. Guenther Roth and Claus Wittich, trans. E. Fischoff et al. (Berkeley: University of California Press, 1978), 241.

[9] Marc Ambinder, "Feeling Your Pain," *The Week*, October 2012, http://theweek.com/articles/471681/feeling-pain.

[10] Mehrabian, A. (1972). *Nonverbal communication.* Chicago, IL: Aldine-Atherton

[11] Edgar Dale, *Audio-Visual Methods in Teaching*, 3rd ed. (New York: Dryden, 1969), 107.

[12] Will Thalheimer, "How Much Do People Forget?" Work-Learning Research, Inc. 2010. http://willthalheimer.typepad.com/files/how-much-do-people-forget-v12-14-2010-2.pdf.

[13] Thalheimer, "How Much Do People Forget?" 2010.

[14] Peter Dixon and Marisa Bortolussi, "Construction, Integration, and Mind Wandering in Reading," *Canadian Journal of Experimental Psychology* 67, no. 1 (March 2013): 1-10; Shi Feng, Sidney D'Mello, and Arthur C. Graesser, "Mind Wandering While Reading Easy and Difficult Texts," *Psychonomic Bulletin and Review* 20, no. 3 (June 2013): 586–92; James Farley, Evan F. Risko, and Alan Kingstone, "Everyday Attention and Lecture Retention: The Effects of Time, Fidgeting, and Mind Wandering," *Frontiers in Psychology* 4 (September 2013): 619; Sophie I. Lindquist and John P. McLean, "Daydreaming and its Correlates in an Educational Environment," *Learning and Individual Differences* 21, no. 2 (April 2011): 158-67; Michael J. Kane and Jennifer C. McVay, "What Mind Wandering Reveals About Executive-Control Abilities and Failures," *Current*

Directions in Psychological Science 21, no. 2 (Oct. 2012): 358-54; Jennifer A. Cowley, "Off Task Thinking Types and Performance Decrements During Simulated Automobile Driving," *Proceedings of the Human Factors and Ergonomics Society Annual Meeting* 57, no. 1 (September 2013): 1214-1218.

[15] Benjamin Baird et al 2012, "Inspired by Distraction: Mind Wandering Facilitates Creative Incubation," *Psychological Science* 23 (2012): 1117-22; Florence J.M. Ruby et al, "How Self-Generated Thought Shapes Mood—The Relation between Mind-Wandering and Mood Depends on the Socio-Temporal Content of Thoughts," *PLoS One* (2013): 8; Roy F. Baumeister and E. J. Masicampo, "Conscious Thought is for Facilitating Social and Cultural Interactions: How Mental Simulations Serve the Animal–culture Interface," *Psychological Review* 117, no. 3 (July 2010): 945-71.

[16] See, e.g., Jonathan Smallwood and Jonathan W. Schooler, "The Restless Mind," *Psychological Bulletin* 132 (2006), 946; Chin-Teng Lin et al, "Mind-Wandering Tends to Occur under Low Perceptual Demands during Driving," *Scientific Reports* 6 (2016): 1.

[17] Matthew A. Killingsworth and Daniel T. Gilbert, "A Wandering Mind Is an Unhappy Mind," *Science* 330, no. 6006 (2010): 932.

[18] See, e.g., Mark Green, "The Six Laws of Attention," 2008, http://www.visualexpert.com/Resources/lawsofattention.html; Michael St. Pierre et al, *Crisis Management in Acute Care Settings* (New York: Springer Science and Business Media, 2011), 143.

[19] Carmine Gallo, *Talk Like Ted: The 9 Public-Speaking Secrets of the World's Top Minds* (New York: St. Martin's Press, 2014), 184.

[20] James Hartley and Ivor K. Davies, "Note-taking: A Critical Review," *Programmed Learning and Educational Technology* 15 (1967): 207-224.

[21] Nico Bunzeck and Emrah Duzel, "Absolute Coding of Stimulus Novelty in the Human Substantia Nigra/VTA," *Neuron* 51 (August 2006): 369-79.

[22] Edward E. Smith and Stephen M. Kosslyn, *Cognitive Psychology: Mind and Brain* (Upper Saddle River, N.J.: Pearson/Prentice Hall, 2007); E. Bruce Goldstein, *Cognitive Psychology: Connecting Mind, Research and Everyday Experience,* 4th Ed. (Stamford, CT: Cengage, 2014).

[23] Smith and Kosslyn, *Cognitive Psychology*, 243-44; George Miller, "The Magical Number Seven, Plus or Minus Two: Some Limits on Our Capacity for Processing Information," *Psychological Review* 63, no. 2 (1956): 343-52.

[24] Nelson Cowan, "The Magical Number 4 in Short-term Memory: A Reconsideration of Mental Storage Capacity," *Behavioral and Brain Sciences* 24 (2001): 87-185.

[25] Cong Li, "Primacy Effect or Recency Effect? A Long-term Memory Test of Super Bowl Commercials," *Journal of Consumer Behavior* 9, no. 1 (January/February 2010): 32-44.

[26] W. Scott Terry, "Serial Position Effects in Recall of Television Commercials," *Journal of General Psychology* 132, no. 2 (2005): 151-63.

[27] Carmen Simon, "What Do We Remember from PowerPoint Presentations?" February 2013, http://www.reximedia.com/remember-powerpoint-presentations/#.VzTf7hUrIgo.

[28] Lionel Standing, Jerry Conezio, and Ralph Norman Haber, "Perception and Memory for Pictures: Single-trial Learning of 2500 Visual Stimuli," *Psychonomic Science* 19, no. 2 (1970): 73-74.

[29] Allan Paivio and Kalman Csapo, "Picture Superiority in Free Recall: Imagery or Dual Coding?" *Cognitive Psychology* 5 (1973): 176-206.

[30] Rik Pieters and Michel Wedel, "Attention Capture and Transfer in Advertising: Brand, Pictorial, and Text-Size Effects," *Journal of Marketing* 68 (April 2004): 36-50.

[31] Douglas L. Nelson, Valerie S. Reed, and John R. Walling, "Pictorial Superiority Effect," *Journal of Experimental Psychology: Human Learning and Memory* 2, no. 5 (1976): 523-28.

[32] Allan Paivio, *Imagery and Verbal Processes* (New York: Holt, Rinehart, and Winston, 1971).

[33] See, e.g., Paul Chandler and John Sweller, "Cognitive Load Theory and the Format of Instruction," *Cognition and Instruction* 8, no. 4 (1991): 293-332.

[34] Roxana Moreno and Richard E. Mayer, "Verbal Redundancy in Multimedia Learning: When Reading Helps Listening," *Journal of Educational Psychology* 94, no. 1 (2002): 156-63.

[35] Robert A. Bartsch and Kristi M. Cobern, "Effectiveness of PowerPoint Presentations in Lectures," *Computers and Education* 41, no. 1 (2003): 77-86.

[36] Alden Hatch, *Buckminster Fuller: At Home in the Universe* (New York: Dell, 1976).

[37] Clance, P. R., & Imes, S. A. (1978). The impostor phenomenon in high achieving women: Dynamics and therapeutic intervention.

[38] Jeffrey A. Linder et al., "Time of Day and the Decision to Prescribe Antibiotics," *JAMA Internal Medicine* 174 (2014): 2029-2031.

[39] Rollnick S., & Miller, W.R. (1995). What is motivational interviewing? *Behavioural and Cognitive Psychotherapy*, *23*, 325-334 Psychotherapy: Theory, Research, and Practice, 15, 241–247.

[40] Autumn Hostetter, "When Do Gestures Communicate? A Meta-Analysis," *Psychological Bulletin* 137, no. 2 (2011): 297-315.

[41] Susan Wagner Cook, Ryan G. Duffy, and Kimberly M. Fenn, "Consolidation and Transfer of Learning After Observing Hand Gesture," *Child Development* 84, no. 6 (November/December 2013): 1863-1871.

[42] Sheena Finlayson et al., "Effects of the Restriction of Hand Gestures on Disfluency," *Proceedings of DiSS'03* (September 2003): 21-24.

[43] Claire Conway, "Evidence for Adaptive Design in Human Gaze Preference," *Proceedings of the Royal Society: Biological Sciences* 275, no. 1630 (2008): 63-69.

[44] Rick Fry and Gene Smith, "The Effects of Feedback and Eye Contact on Performance of a Digit-Coding Task," *Social Psychology* 96, no. 1 (1975): 145-46; Chris Fullwood and Gwyneth Doherty-Sneddon, "Effect of Gazing at the Camera During a Video Link on Recall," *Applied Ergonomics* 37 (2006): 167-75.

[45] Derek H. Kelley and Joan Gorham, "Effects of Immediacy on Recall of Information," *Communication Education* 37, no. 3 (1988): 198-207.

[46] *Google, s.v.,* "anxiety," accessed June 14, 2016, https://www.google.com/webhp?sourceid=chrome-instant&ion=1&espv=2&ie=UTF-8#q=anxiety+define

[47] Stanley Schachter and Jerome Singer, "Cognitive, Social, and Physiological Determinants of Emotional State," *Psychological Review* 69, no. 5 (September 1962): 379-99.

[48] Gary Goodwin, "Squeeze Stress Away. Thank you, Dorothy Sarnoff," Wild Stress, last modified July 6, 2013, https://wildstress.wordpress.com/2013/07/06/squeeze-stress-away-thank-you-dorothy-sarnoff/.

[49] Nancy Duarte, "Structure Your Presentation Like a Story," *Harvard Business Review*, October 31, 2012, https://hbr.org/2012/10/structure-your-presentation-li.

[50] See, e.g., Leslie Belknap, "Minimize the Extraneous Load of Your Presentations," Ethos3 Communications, 20 January 2015, https://www.ethos3.com/2015/01/how-to-minimize-the-extraneous-load-of-your-presentations/.

[51] Ton de Jong, "Cognitive Load Theory, Educational Research, and Instructional Design: Some Food for Thought," *Instructional Science* 38, no. 2 (March 2010): 105-134.

[52] Annie Murphy Paul, "Your Brain on Fiction," *New York Times*, March 17, 2012.

[53] Paul J. Zak, "Why Your Brain Loves Good Storytelling," *Harvard Business Review*, 28 October 2014, https://hbr.org/2014/10/why-your-brain-loves-good-storytelling/.

[54] Zak, "Why Your Brain," 2014.

[55] U.S. Department of Health and Human Services, "Quick Guide to Health Literacy," accessed June 10, 2016, http://health.gov/communication/literacy/quickguide/factsbasic.htm.

[56] Roland McCraty, *Science of the Heart: Exploring the Role of the Heart in Human Performance*, Volume 2, HeartMath Institute, 2015

[57] Doc Childre, Howard Martin, Deborah Rozman and Rollin McCraty, *Heart Intelligence: Connecting with the Intuitive Guidance of the Heart*, Waterfront Press, 2016

[58] Joseph Luft and Harrington Ingham, "The Johari Window, a Graphic Model of Interpersonal Awareness," in *Proceedings of the Western Training Laboratory in Group Development* (Los Angeles: University of California, Los Angeles, 1955).

[59] Kenneth Savitsky and Thomas Gilovich, "The Illusion of Transparency and the Alleviation of Speech Anxiety," *Journal of Experimental Social Psychology* 39, no. 6 (2003): 618-25.

[60] Mihaly Csikszentmihalyi, *Beyond Boredom and Anxiety* (San Francisco: Jossey-Bass, 1975), 36.

[61] Mihaly Csikszentmihalyi, "Artistic Problems and Their Solutions: An Exploration of Creativity in the Arts." PhD diss., University of Chicago, 1965; Jacob W. Getzels and Mihaly Csikszentmihalyi, *The Creative Vision* (New York: Wiley, 1976).

[62] Mihaly Csikszentmihalyi, Reed Larson, and Suzanne Prescott, "The Ecology of Adolescent Activity and Experience," *Journal of Youth and Adolescence* 6 (1977): 181-294; Mihaly Csikszentmihalyi and Judith LeFevre, "Optimal Experience in Work and Leisure," *Journal of Personality and Social Psychology* 56, no. 5 (May 1989): 815-22.

[63] Mihaly Csikszentmihalyi. *Flow: The Psychology of Optimal Experience* (New York: Harper and Row, 1990), 71.

[64] Brooke Macnamara, David Moreau, and David Z. Hambrick, "The Relationship Between Deliberate Practice and Performance in Sports: A Meta-Analysis," *Perspectives on Psychological Science* 11 (May 2016): 333-50.